UNITED BY NUMBERS

£514.9 MILLION
TOTAL CLUB DEBT AS OF SEPT 2022

3 EUROPEAN CUPS

20
LEAGUE TITLES

12
FA CUPS

76,000
OLD TRAFFORD'S CAPACITY

963
RYAN GIGGS' RECORD APPEARANCE TALLY

2,223
PREMIER LEAGUE GOALS SCORED

38
CHAMPIONS LEAGUE GOALS SCORED BY RUUD VAN NISTELROOY, MORE THAN ANY OTHER UNITED PLAYER

9-0
UNITED'S BIGGEST EVER VICTORY
(VS IPSWICH, 4 MARCH 1995)

1,176
PREMIER LEAGUE GAMES PLAYED

717
PREMIER
LEA...

,692
DAYS
...LEX FERGUSON
...ENT AS UNITED MANAGER

253
WAYNE ROONEY'S RECORD GOAL TALLY

£3.7 BILLION
CURRENT VALUE OF
THE CLUB

*STATS ACCURATE AS OF 14/02/2023

GLORY GLORY MAN UTD!

Step inside the Theatre of Dreams, home to one of the greatest clubs in sport and witness to countless stirring comebacks, flashes of genius and last-gasp winners. Yet while the hallowed turf of Old Trafford has been graced by legends such as Charlton, Best, Cantona and Rooney, it was not always Manchester United's fortress. In fact, the club wasn't always known as it is today. Welcome to the story of the railway workers' team that would become a mega-club.

Within these pages you will meet the men who founded United, relive the glory days of the Busby Babes and commemorate the tragedy that changed the club forever. You will also take to the field alongside United's greatest players, celebrate its finest moments, and find out what may lie ahead now that Erik ten Hag is at the helm. With Ronaldo having departed for a second time, is the path now clear for United's no-nonsense Dutch manager to impose his pressing style and lead England's biggest club back to the summit?

W0006980

FUTURE

THE STORY OF
MAN UTD

Future PLC Quay House, The Ambury, Bath, BA1 1UA

Bookazine Editorial
Editor **Charles Ginger**
Designer **Perry Wardell-Wicks**
Senior Art Editor **Andy Downes**
Head of Art & Design **Greg Whitaker**
Editorial Director **Jon White**

FourFourTwo Editorial
Editor **James Andrew**
Deputy Editor **Matthew Ketchell**
Art Director **Anthony Moore**
Chief Sub Editor **Gregg Davies**
Senior Staff Writer **Chris Flanagan**
Staff Writer **Mark White**
Staff Writer **Ed McCambridge**
Staff Writer **Ryan Dabbs**

Cover images
Getty Images
All copyrights and trademarks are recognised and respected

Advertising
Media packs are available on request
Commercial Director **Clare Dove**

International
Head of Print Licensing **Rachel Shaw**
licensing@futurenet.com
www.futurecontenthub.com

Circulation
Head of Newstrade **Tim Mathers**

Production
Head of Production **Mark Constance**
Production Project Manager **Matthew Eglinton**
Advertising Production Manager **Joanne Crosby**
Digital Editions Controller **Jason Hudson**
Production Managers **Keely Miller, Nola Cokely,
Vivienne Calvert, Fran Twentyman**

Printed in the UK

Distributed by Marketforce, 5 Churchill Place, Canary Wharf, London, E14 5HU
www.marketforce.co.uk Tel: 0203 787 9001

FourFourTwo Presents: The Story of Man Utd Second Edition (SBZ5142)
© 2023 Future Publishing Limited

FUTURE Connectors.
Creators.
Experience
Makers.

Future plc is a public
company quoted on the
London Stock Exchange
(symbol: FUTR)
www.futureplc.com

Chief Executive **Zillah Byng-Thorne**
Non-Executive Chairman **Richard Huntingford**
Chief Financial and Strategy Officer **Penny Ladkin-Brand**

Tel +44 (0)1225 442 244

Part of the
FourFourTwo
bookazine series

Widely
Recycled

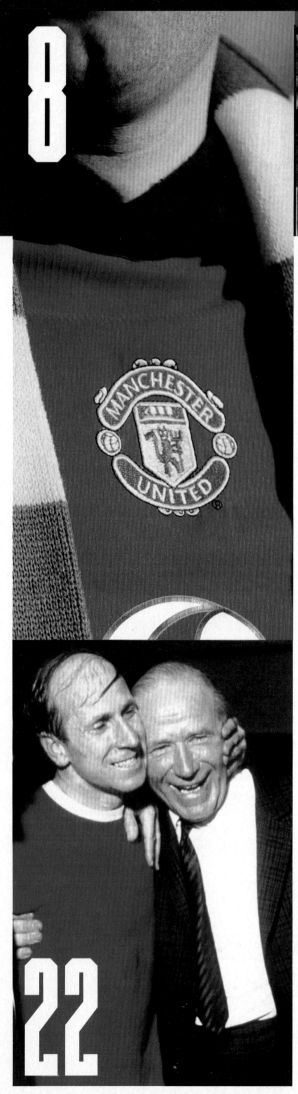

8

CONT

22

8 From the Heath to the Theatre of Dreams
The making of English football's biggest club

12 The Busby Babes
How a youthful revolution transformed United's fortunes

18 Munich
Inside the disaster that claimed 23 lives and devastated a club

22 Champions of Europe at last
Rising from the ashes, United marched to glory in 1968

26 United they fall
As the golden years faded, United found themselves adrift

28 When United stopped Liverpool doing the treble
22 years before United did it, Liverpool so nearly clinched the big three

34 That's entertainment
It wasn't always plain sailing with Big Ron, but it was never dull either

36 The man from Aberdeen
In late 1986 a struggling United turned to a fiery Scot to save them

42 The Class of '92
Meet the legendary members of this iconic clutch of young stars

46 The 50 greatest Red Devils of all time
We list the finest United stars ever to pull on that famous red jersey

60 Eric Cantona
Tantrums. Trawlers. Tricks. Trophies. How Cantona transformed United

74 United dominate the '90s
A first league title in 26 years acted as a springboard to further glory

80 The impossible dream
It began as a joke between team-mates, but by May 1999 the Red Devils
were on the cusp of immortality

ENTS

12

46

86

Images Getty Images, Wiki Images

86 The new millennium
For United, the world was never going to be enough, and as the 21st century unfolded Fergie's charges were ready to fight for more silverware

88 Wenger vs Fergie
By the summer of '96 Fergie ruled as English football's undisputed king. And then a pioneering French manager took the reins at Arsenal...

94 Ten years of the Glazers
We look at the impact of the first decade of Glazer ownership and why their tenure at the club may soon be over

102 Fergie's double winners
The 2007–08 season would begin with victory over Chelsea, and it would end in similar fashion on a famous night in a rain-soaked Moscow

106 Rio Ferdinand
The former United stalwart discusses winning it all at Old Trafford

112 United's fight to return to the top
Fergie's departure was always going to leave a massive void, but few expected United to fall quite so far without his guiding hand

118 She Devils
They may be late to the game, but United's women are certainly making up for lost time

120 The rise and fall of Ronaldo
They say never go back, and perhaps, given how everything ended, it would have been better if CR7 hadn't

126 Dutch courage: The Erik ten Hag era
He's clearing out the deadwood, imposing a fluid, attacking style of play, and he is determined to end the era of City dominance. Could United's

FROM THE HEATH TO THE THEATRE OF DREAMS

Starting life as a railway side playing on a mud patch in Newton Heath, the world's biggest football club took a few years to become Manchester United

Words Rob Clark

The club that was to become one of the biggest and most successful in the world started life inauspiciously in 1878 as Newton Heath LYR (Lancashire and Yorkshire Railway). Their original aim was no loftier than providing railway workers with some exercise and entertainment at the end of a hard day's labour. At that time, in parts of the newly industrialised Manchester, average life expectancy was as little as 35; many people's everyday lives consisted of work and drink, and not much else. As it is now, so it was then – the managerial class weren't acting out of altruism when they started Newton Heath so much as trying to get a few more productive years out of their workforce.

Although the newly formed club did play matches, they were mostly against other 'railway' teams and as there was no league or formal structure to the sport at that time, results have not been recorded, or only sporadically in local newspapers. It wasn't until 1892 that Newton Heath (by then they had dropped the 'LYR', though in truth the majority of their players were still employed by the railway) first entered the League. By then it had already been running for five seasons, and for the 1892-93 season it was expanded to two divisions to accommodate growing interest in the sport.

Newton Heath's debut league match, on 3 September 1892, was at Blackburn Rovers' famous Ewood Park ground, a tough opener against one of the top teams of the day who had already won the FA Cup five times by then. Rovers also boasted in Jack Southworth an England international who scored 97 goals in 108 games for his club. Predictably, Newton Heath lost 4-3, although they at least gave a good account of themselves after conceding three goals in the first ten minutes. They suffered another, heavier, 4-0 defeat to Rovers in the first round of the FA Cup.

Newton Heath were not, at that stage, quite ready for League football, and won only six of their 30 matches that season (a further six were drawn). However, their first home match was a notable success: they beat Wolverhampton Wanderers 10-1. Wanderers were a good side who would go on to win the FA Cup that season, but they were outclassed on the day, with a hat-trick from the club's first great goalscorer, Bob Donaldson.

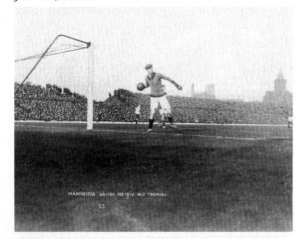

"NEWTON HEATH FINISHED ROCK BOTTOM OF THE TABLE IN THEIR FIRST SEASON"

Other successes were few and far between though, and Newton Heath finished rock bottom of the table in their first season, five points adrift of Accrington. No rules had been set in place regarding relegation and promotion so it was decided that the bottom three clubs in the First Division would play off against the top three in the Second Division. That meant a match against Small Heath (later to become Birmingham City), which resulted in a 1-1 draw. The replay went in Newton Heath's favour, 5-2, thus securing their place in the top flight for their second season. Interestingly the other two bottom-three clubs, Accrington and Notts County, both lost their play-offs, to Sheffield United and Darwen respectively, and were relegated.

Off the pitch, there were problems too. LYR told the club that they would have to leave the North Road ground – not in itself bad news as it was not much of a ground, lacking even changing facilities (the players usually trudged off to the Three Crowns pub some half a mile away to get changed), but it meant leaving behind two stands for spectators that the club had bought. Attempts to move the stands ended in failure, so they had to be left behind.

That first season was to prove a short-lived respite for Newton Heath. The following season they again finished bottom of the table, and this time there was no play-off (or test match as they were then called) to save them. They went down to the Second Division, and would spend the following 12 seasons there. The most notable event of those otherwise unremarkable 12 years came in 1902 when local

Above Welsh winger Billy Meredith (left, against Queen's Park Rangers in the 1908 Charity Shield) was the game's first superstar
Left top Action from the first-ever match at Old Trafford, 19 February 1910
Left bottom The Newton Heath team in 1892

businessman John Henry Davies, a wealthy brewery owner who was also married to the Tate & Lyle Group heiress, was persuaded to invest in the club. Davies was both rich and influential and he brought with him three further investors, each of the men putting £500 in. Davies moved the club to Bank Street, changed its name to Manchester United (they no longer played near, nor had any connections with, Newton Heath), and switched their green-and-gold shirts to the famous red ones. The club we now know as United had been properly born. Fans still occasionally pay homage to the club's original strip by sporting green-and-gold shirts, hats and scarves.

The move to Bank Street resulted in a huge increase in the number of fans attending each match. The average crowd size more than doubled, from around 4,500 who went to Newton Heath (estimates are a little variable as there was no standard mechanism for counting the numbers through the turnstiles in those days) to almost 10,000 in the club's first season as United. Even then, United fans were demanding, though. They wanted to see their club do better than amble around in the middle of the Second Division. A financial scandal in which both secretary James West and captain Harry Stafford were embroiled saw the former resign and the latter be banned from the game for five years, but this actually had the fortuitous result of bringing Ernest Mangnall to the club (see below).

The surprise acquisition of the Manchester City forward line was a masterstroke by Mangnall. Billy Meredith, the Welsh winger, was the sport's first superstar, and his capture was a coup of the same order as the signing of Eric Cantona following a casual enquiry 86 years later. He was also the first in a long line of wingers at the club who have captured the fans' imaginations, from Gordon Hill and Steve

Above left
United fans still pay homage to the original shirts worn by Newton Heath by sporting the green-and-gold colours

Above right
Old Trafford was one of the finest stadiums of its time and was packed when it hosted the 1911 FA Cup Final replay (Bradford City beat Newcastle United 1-0)

Coppell to Jesper Olsen and Ryan Giggs, and the start of a style of play which has been synonymous with United ever since.

Now United had a fearsome attacking line-up to bolt onto a solid defence, and in the 1907-08 season they took the league by storm, winning their first ten games and leading from gun to tape, ultimately winning the league by nine points. Mangnall delivered another league title three seasons later and a first FA Cup (arguably the more sought-after trophy in those days) in 1909.

Buoyed by their growing success, Davies had invested £60,000 into the club to build a new stadium at Old Trafford, a vast sum of money at that time. Their first match at the new stadium took place on 19 February 1910; although the day was partially spoilt by visitors Liverpool, of all teams, who won 4-3, it mattered little; the Theatre of Dreams had arrived.

Like its owner and manager, United's stadium was years ahead of its time. Featuring a huge stand on one side, rows of wooden benches on another and terraces offering standing room for 80,000 fans, it was the most impressive stadium of its era. It also boasted a pitch with decent drainage, so instead of the mud bath that Newton Heath used to play on there was a beautiful bit of turf which further encouraged the players to play a passing game.

Although Mangnall and Davies fell out – over money, as is often the case between owners and managers – and the former resigned in a fit of pique, the pieces were in place for United to experience its first 'golden age'.

Little did those associated with the club realise that it would be over 40 years until their next league title and almost as long before another FA Cup triumph.

THE SEEDS OF SUCCESS

Ernest Mangnall was the first great United manager, both in terms of the way his team played and the trophies they won

Ernest Mangnall was the highly rated secretary of Burnley and a man fully aware of his own worth. He was also a man of strong opinions, his main opinion being that he was right – in everything. But he was also a visionary. Mangnall saw United's glorious future, not only in this country but in Europe; under his stewardship the club embarked on its first continental tour, to Prague, Vienna and Budapest.

Mangnall liked to portray himself as a man ahead of his time and, as a consequence, the only person able to handle all aspects of the intricate task of running a football club. To give him his due, though, he revolutionised training, emphasising the importance of fitness and demanding their all from his players. He foresaw the famous Brian Clough approach to management of listening to opinions from everybody – before deciding that he had

been right all along. He commanded respect and demanded total control over every aspect of the club.

It's easy to forget now, but Mangnall was initially a safety-first guiding hand, fielding a rugged defence and imbuing the team with a philosophy of conceding fewer goals than they scored. But that all changed in 1906. Neighbours Manchester City were punished for financial irregularities by being forced to sell all their players. Rivals turned up for the much-anticipated auction at the Queen's Hotel in Manchester only to discover that Mangnall had already persuaded Alex Turnbull, Billy Meredith, Jimmy Bannister and Herbert Burgess to sign with United. All the transfers were free and constituted four of the five City forwards who had been terrorising the league the previous season. Now United had a team capable of putting others to the sword.

THE BUSBY BABES

The arrival of Matt Busby and his 'Babes' heralded a golden age for United and introduced a youth policy and playing style that survive to this day

Words Rob Clark

The years between World War I and World War II were ones of turmoil for United; eight of them (across two different periods) were spent in Division Two and only once in 20 seasons did they finish in the top half of Division One – in 1925–26, when they scrapped their way to ninth (out of 22 teams) and reached their only FA Cup semi-final of the interwar years. Their most important match of that period did not even come in the top flight but in the 1933–34 season when they had to win on the last day at Millwall's Den to avoid relegation to the Third Division North. They did so, 2-0, and never again came close to dropping down that far, but it was a salutary lesson for all involved with the club.

The lesson appeared to have been learnt, and the club decided that the answer to their dire financial straits lay in putting in place a structure for producing their own players. Thus was born the Manchester United Junior Athletic Club (MUJAC), and bringing through youth team players became a raison d'être. Johnny Carey and Stan Pearson were two of the first to benefit from MUJAC, and both went on to make over 300 appearances for the club. Carey had a formidable career in football, becoming a coach and working at Blackburn Rovers, Everton and in his native Republic of Ireland. Pearson was a United fan and lived just hundreds of yards away from the ground. He scored 148 goals in league and cup, putting him 12th in the list of all-time United goalscorers. If he had done nothing else in his football career, Pearson would always have been a fan favourite at Old Trafford for his hat-trick against Liverpool in a 5-0 win on 11 September 1946 – the last hat-trick against Liverpool until Dimitar Berbatov in 2010.

At that time United were using Maine Road as a venue for their home games as Old Trafford had suffered extensive bomb damage during the war. From the ashes of the Theatre of Dreams and the underperforming team of the 1920s and 1930s was born one of the greatest club sides of all time. And the architect of that building work was one Matt Busby.

Back in 1930, the club's unofficial fixer and scout, Louis Rocca, had recommended the club buy a 21-year-old Manchester City winger named Matt Busby, but the club couldn't raise the £150 transfer fee demanded by their city rivals. The deal never happened, but Rocca and Busby stayed in touch, and when he decided to call time on his playing career and move into management, Rocca persuaded him to come to United. Chairman James Gibson had the foresight to agree to Busby's appointment, even though Busby demanded a level of control over the club that was almost unheard of in those days.

The final piece of the jigsaw fitted into place when Busby bumped into Welshman Jimmy Murphy at an army football match in Bari, Italy, in spring 1945. Recalling the many times they had met on the field, Busby had no hesitation in offering Murphy the job of his assistant. The Busby era, aided and abetted by Murphy, began on 1 October 1945.

United started the post-war years with a bang, finishing second four seasons out of five (they were fourth in the other) and adding the 1948 FA Cup to their honours. That was the famous 4-2 win over a Blackpool side featuring Stan Mortensen and Stanley Matthews. Blackpool led twice in the game, but goals from Jack Rowley (his second), then from Pearson and John Anderson in the final ten minutes, were enough to bring the cup back to Manchester.

Four years later they claimed their first league title in over 40 years, but that was more a last hurrah than the dawning of a new age. Even as they won the 1951-52 league title, the ever-prescient Busby could

see his team were ageing and were in need of new blood. Of the 24 players who made league appearances in the 1952 championship-winning side, only six remained by the time of their next win, four years later. In the place of departing giants such as Carey, Pearson, Rowley and Allenby Chilton came names to conjure with: Roger Byrne, Eddie Colman, Tommy Taylor, Dennis Viollet, Bill Foulkes and, of course, Duncan Edwards. The Busby Babes.

The birth of the Busby Babes can be tracked back to the unlikely setting of Kilmarnock, on 28 October 1953, in a friendly to mark the installation of floodlights at the Scottish club's Rugby Park ground. Busby decided he would omit both Rowley and Pearson in favour of Viollet and Jackie Blanchflower, both just 20. Taylor also played, and Kilmarnock FC historian John Livingstone recalls his father saying that Taylor was 'the best centre-forward he had ever seen'. The youngsters played well in a 3-0 win and Busby decided to give youth its head. Over the following couple of seasons he did occasionally have second thoughts as to whether he had gone too far down the youth route

Top Stan Pearson (out of shot) scores the third United goal in the 1948 FA Cup win over Blackpool
Left Wartime bomb damage rendered Old Trafford unusable until 1949
Top right Duncan Edwards signs an autograph for a young fan in 1958
Bottom right United keeper Ray Wood is injured in a clash with Aston Villa's Peter McParland during the 1957 FA Cup Final

"UNITED STARTED THE POST-WAR YEARS WITH A BANG, FINISHING SECOND FOUR SEASONS OUT OF FIVE (THEY WERE FOURTH IN THE OTHER) AND ADDING THE 1948 FA CUP TO THEIR HONOURS"

"GOALSCORER SUPREME, TAYLOR NOTCHED 131 GOALS IN 191 APPEARANCES AND WAS STILL ONLY 26 WHEN HE DIED"

too quickly. But whenever he wavered, Murphy was quick to reassure him that he was doing the right thing.

The Busby Babes were a bunch of young players who were so exceptional it's difficult to assess quite how good they were some 70 years on, especially as so little TV footage of them remains. But what we do have is accounts of matches they played and, above all, the opinions of fellow stars who played against and alongside them.

Roger Byrne was the captain and a born leader, described by Bobby Charlton as "somehow set apart... with a wonderful confidence in his own talent and he passed it on so effortlessly. You only had to see him at work to feel a surge of belief spreading through the team." John Doherty, a teammate and frequently a roommate, said simply that Byrne was "as good a left-back as has ever played the game. Players like Roger operate in their own world. You just have to let them get on with it, and then marvel at what they achieve."

Byrne arrived at United a little bit before most of his fellow 'Babes', which perhaps gave him a natural authority, but he was swiftly joined by Eddie Colman. Nicknamed 'Snakehips' for his sinewy movement, Colman was the heart and soul of the team. If Byrne was a bit of a loner away from the pitch, Colman was an extrovert who wanted to live life to the full. Murphy said of him that "he was an original. He had things you couldn't teach," while Bill Foulkes – hardly known for his gushing appraisals of fellow players – said "he always made you feel happy to be alive. He was somebody you couldn't begin to replace."

And what of Tommy Taylor? Goalscorer supreme, Taylor notched 131 goals in 191 appearances. Still only 26 when he died, Taylor could reasonably have expected to play for another four seasons at the highest level. If he'd maintained a similar scoring rate, he would have

Above Jimmy Murphy (left) was an indispensable assistant to Matt Busby for many years
Top left Tommy Taylor, David Pegg and Roger Byrne enjoy some downtime
Above left Matt Busby at training with (left to right) Wilf McGuinness, Dennis Viollet, David Pegg and Tommy Taylor

ended up close to being United's all-time leading goalscorer. As he also notched 16 in his 19 England games, it is clear that Taylor was a goalscorer on a par with the very best of the best. Taylor was actually happy playing for Barnsley, but his hometown club desperately needed the money a transfer to United would bring, and he turned out to be the signing that crystallised the buzz that was building at the club. Murphy described him as "the final piece in our jigsaw", while Jackie Blanchflower, perhaps Taylor's closest friend at the club, recalled that, "[We] were having trouble with the centre-forward position before Tommy Taylor arrived. We needed a big, strong centre-forward and Tommy was ideal."

The hard-working Taylor was a fanatical trainer, and any rough edges he had as a result of not coming up through United's junior ranks were quickly ironed out. Teammate Ian Greaves recalled that Taylor was always doing extra heading practice despite already being the best header of the ball at the club. "That was dedication for you. He was never satisfied to be good, he strived to become the best. Tommy Taylor was the best striker I ever saw, never mind having the good fortune to play with."

At the start of the 1955-56 season, Duncan Edwards was on National Service and travelling to and from United games, home or away, from his base in Shrewsbury. Edwards was irreplaceable. His heading ability, talent to play with his back to goal and hold the ball up, his long, raking passes and his dynamic presence galvanised the team in a way that nobody before – or arguably since – had done. Bobby Charlton has always maintained that "I totally believe Duncan Edwards was the best player I ever saw or am likely to see. Yes, I know all about Maradona, Best, Law and the others, but if you asked great players like Tom Finney and Stanley Matthews who was the greatest, they would tell you, as they did me, they hadn't seen anything like Duncan."

Back-to-back league titles in 1955-56 and 1956-57 were just reward for a United team that swept all before them. They also reached the FA Cup final in consecutive seasons. In 1957, they disappointingly lost 2-1 to Aston Villa, though the score doesn't

ARSENAL OUTGUNNED

In their last league match before their fateful trip, we saw all that was brightest and best of United in a nine-goal thriller

Defending their title, United had not started the 1957-58 season in quite the same dominating form as they had shown in the previous two seasons. In an attempt to fire up his side, Matt Busby had introduced Bobby Charlton, Kenny Morgans and the mercurial Eddie Colman, and they had started to buzz again. On 1 February 1958, they travelled to Highbury for what became an extraordinary match. United went 3-0 up thanks to Edwards (above, arms outstretched), Charlton and Taylor but relaxed too soon and Arsenal hit back with three of their own through David Herd and a Jimmy Bloomfield double. As an end-to-end battle developed, United again went ahead through Viollet and another from Taylor. But still the Gunners weren't finished and Derek Tapscott made it 4-5. That was the end of the scoring, but not the end of the excitement as further chances came and went for both sides. The 63,578 crowd must have been disappointed at the result but can't help having been thrilled by the action. The match was given added poignancy as it was United's last league game before their ill-fated trip to Belgrade; on their return they unsurprisingly lost eight of their remaining 13 fixtures, and with it the chance of a hat-trick of league titles.

begin to tell the story of the match. Only a few minutes into the game, a strong challenge from Villa's Peter McParland on goalkeeper Ray Wood led to the latter being carried off; in the days before substitutes were allowed this meant United played almost the whole match with ten men – and with Jackie Blanchflower in goal! The following year, having gutsily survived post-Munich ties against West Bromwich Albion and Fulham – both via replays – United succumbed 2-0 to Bolton Wanderers in the final. Both goals were scored by Nat Lofthouse for a Bolton side that boasted five internationals; United fielded just two players who had appeared in the previous year's final.

Of course the bigger story was Busby's insistence that they enter the European Cup. It seems difficult to imagine now, but the Football League were very much against the competition and even tried to prevent United from taking part.

"Football has become a world game and this is where the future of the game lies," declared Busby. "You cannot make progress standing still." And so it was that United became the first English club to take part, and they quickly had an impact.

Wins over Anderlecht, Borussia Dortmund and Athletic Bilbao in their first season brought a semi-final against giants Real Madrid. A 3-1 defeat at the Bernabéu in front of a reported 120,000 crowd made United's task hard; two first-half goals from the Spanish side at Old Trafford put the tie beyond any real doubt. But the home team showed glimpses of what they had to offer, and goals from Taylor and Charlton at least gained them parity on the night. The Spanish side used the counterattack cleverly and weren't above some serious gamesmanship in milking every foul, committing plenty themselves and repeatedly kicking the ball away whenever the home team were awarded a free kick.

But United learned valuable lessons about European campaigns, which looked like they might bear fruit the following year. With Madrid going on to lift the trophy via a comfortable 2-0 win over Fiorentina, it was clear that United were not that far off the pace. "When I led Manchester United into Europe," said Busby, "some people called me a visionary, others a reactionary, while a few thought me just plain awkward and stubborn. Certainly I was eager to be part of this new European challenge."

The following season they again reached the semi-finals with wins over Shamrock Rovers, Dukla Prague and Red Star Belgrade. Astonishingly, they even beat AC Milan 2-1 in the first leg of the semi, just three months after Munich, but they ran out of steam in the return leg, losing 4-0. The terrible events in Munich meant that United would have to wait another decade before finally bringing home the trophy that Busby was so insistent they play for.

Below Billy Whelan, Dennis Viollet and Ray Wood engage in an impromptu training session

MUNICH

6 February 1958 was the day a team died, as the Busby Babes were wiped out in one of
the greatest tragedies in football

Words Rob Clark

Images Getty Images

Our opening image shows Manchester United lining up before the start of the European Cup quarter-final second-leg match versus Red Star Belgrade in the Yugoslavian capital. A 3-3 draw ensured that they progressed to a semi-final against AC Milan – an opening blitz gave United a 3-0 lead after barely half an hour's play, and although Red Star fought back, they couldn't find the fourth goal that would have forced another game (there was no 'away goals' rule in those days).

Hours later, five of the United players who'd featured in the match were dead. So were teammates David Pegg, Billy Whelan and Geoff Bent. Jackie Blanchflower and Johnny Berry would survive but never played football again. Dennis Viollet, Kenny Morgans and Ray Wood were never as good again. As Morgans was to tell *The Daily Mail* on the 50th anniversary of the crash, "I stayed for two more years but I wasn't really interested. I missed the boys so much I just didn't seem to care."

The Munich air disaster wasn't just a footballing tragedy: it was a human one. An avoidable crash, it was originally put down to pilot error, but captain James Thain was later exonerated and the crash ascribed to the amount of slushy ice on the runway, which prevented the aeroplane generating sufficient speed for safe take-off. The plane had stopped at the Munich-Riem Airport for refuelling on the way back from Belgrade, where the weather conditions had been good. In Munich they were much more hazardous and should have led to the postponement of the flight home. Indeed, Duncan Edwards had sent a telegram to his landlady with words to that effect.

But the English Football League had never been enthusiastic supporters of Matt Busby's determination to enter the European Cup, and they weren't prepared to make any fixture concessions to the English champions. With that concern as the backdrop, and a desire to prove to League Secretary Alan Hardaker that they could compete in Europe without compromising their (rapidly improving) form at home, the decision was taken to try to get home. It was a fateful one.

As the Airspeed Ambassador British European Airways flight 609 attempted take-off, captain Thain and co-pilot Kenneth Rayment realised they weren't going to get up into the air. The aircraft careered through the airport perimeter fence and hit a house (fortunately none of the occupants were hurt), which burst into flames. A section of the stricken plane then struck a wooden hut housing a truck filled with fuel, which promptly exploded.

When you see pictures of the wreckage on the runway, what strikes you isn't that so many people died, it's that any survived. The rear section of the plane had sheared off and bits of aircraft were strewn some distance away (Morgans was not discovered until several hours after the crash). A number of the survivors were either too shocked to help or too badly injured to do so – Blanchflower, for example, had one of his arms almost severed in the accident and was also pinned in place by his dead captain, Roger Byrne. However, there were also some stirring stories of heroism. *Daily Mail* photographer Peter Howard helped Albert Scanlon and Ray Wood, who were trapped by debris, and journalist Frank Taylor, whose left arm and right leg were badly broken, as were his collarbone and nine of his

ribs. Thain, meanwhile, had armed himself with fire extinguishers and while telling everyone who was mobile to get clear of the plane was rushing to get the fires under control, in particular the one around the starboard engine that was threatening to blow up.

And then there was Harry Gregg. The story of how Gregg went back time and time again into the smouldering ruins of the plane to find and free his teammates has passed into legend. It is encapsulated in his rescue of Vera Lukić, the pregnant wife of the Yugoslavian air attaché to London, and her baby. Gregg also dragged Charlton and Viollet to safety and sat with a pinned Busby until he could be freed. For many years afterwards Gregg suffered from 'survivor's guilt' and couldn't bear to face the widows and family of his dead teammates. It wasn't until the 40th anniversary of the crash, during a memorial at Manchester Cathedral, that he met Joy Byrne, widow of Roger, who asked him, "Harry Gregg, why have you been torturing yourself for 40 years?"

Gregg's feelings were understandable. At one point he, Murphy and Bill Foulkes walked around the Rechts der Isar Hospital in Munich while Chief Surgeon Georg Maurer gave them an assessment of each man's chances of survival. Johnny Berry, who had a fractured skull and broken jaw, elbow, pelvis and leg, was deemed unlikely to pull through, but he did after spending two months in hospital, during which time he was not informed which of his teammates had died as doctors felt the shock would be too much for his health.

"GREGG DRAGGED CHARLTON AND VIOLLET TO SAFETY AND SAT WITH A PINNED BUSBY UNTIL HE COULD BE FREED"

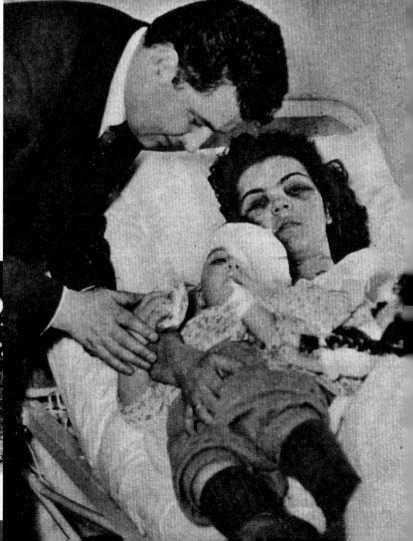

For the 50th anniversary of the Munich air disaster Gregg returned to the scene of the crash for a BBC TV documentary. The Munich-Riem Airport was the city's international airport at that time, but today all that remains are the main terminal building and the control tower, which are protected monuments. There Gregg met Zoran Lukić, son of Vera, with whom she was pregnant at the time. It brought Gregg full circle and perhaps provided the goalkeeper – who always wanted to be remembered for his football rather than his heroism – a measure of closure and peace.

The light in those dark times after the crash was Jimmy Murphy. Murphy hadn't travelled to Belgrade with the team because he doubled as manager of Wales and they had a crucial World Cup qualifier against Israel in Cardiff. Wales' victory saw them qualify, and amid the celebrations Murphy returned to Old Trafford, where Busby's secretary told him of the crash. "She said many people had been killed [including] some of the players... I went into my office and started to cry." But even while he mourned, Murphy was the one who kept the flame alive, who insisted that the club would rise again, and who got them through the matches that followed – the matches no one wanted to play.

Busby, who was so badly injured that he was given the last rites on two separate occasions, urged Murphy to keep the flag flying. Gregg used to say that the greatness of the Busby Babes era was founded on their partnership. In the immediate aftermath of the crash there was so much for Murphy to do, he barely had time to grieve. Not only was Busby in a bad way, but coach Bert Whalley and trainer Tom Curry had also been killed. Murphy said he was in "mental turmoil through sheer sorrow. I also felt completely on my own."

Murphy refused to panic, however, and gradually assessed his options, bringing in England international Ernie Taylor from Blackpool and the tough-tackling half-back Stan Crowther from Aston Villa. United swept into the final of the FA Cup on a wave of emotion, beating Sheffield Wednesday, West Bromwich Albion and Fulham, before running out of steam in the final. There, old foes Bolton Wanderers, boasting five international players, including the great Nat Lofthouse, were too strong, winning 2-0.

A NEW DAWN

While still in hospital, Busby was asked how long it would take to rebuild United and he replied "five years". In 1963, they won the FA Cup and two years later they won the league. Busby's estimated timeframe was uncannily accurate, but in the intervening years the club had acquired two geniuses and several more top players.

Above left Ten days after the crash heavy cranes were still removing pieces of wreckage
Above right Bobby Charlton scores during the fateful game in Belgrade
Left Sir Bobby Charlton, Harry Gregg and Albert Scanlon with Sir Alex Ferguson and current United players at the 50th anniversary memorial service
Below Denis Law looks on as George Best fires past Gordon Banks to give United a 2-1 win over Stoke in 1971

Denis Law had made his name at Manchester City before a big-money move to Torino in 1961. Italian football never suited the Scotsman, however, and in the summer of 1962 he returned to Manchester – and to his previous lodgings and landlady – and became The King. His lightning reflexes and determination to score at all costs brought Law 237 goals from just 404 appearances and third place in the all-time list of United goalscorers. He would have had more but for his regular injuries, which came about in part due to his desire to get into dangerous areas.

Law thrived on being given a free hand to be creative. "We always felt that if the opposition scored one, we could score two; if they scored two, we could get three. It didn't always work out that way, but that was the feeling, and it was all very special for me."

"I think I've found you a genius." So said a telegram to the club from Chief Scout Bob Bishop on seeing a 15-year-old Northern Irish kid playing for Cregagh Boys' Club in Belfast. George Best was a maverick and never easy to manage, much less control, but he was undeniably a footballing genius. Busby said of him, "George Best was gifted with more individual ability than any other player I have seen," while the late, great Graham Taylor added, "What George did was to show that tactics and formations are for the majority of us, while the genius plays the game in a way that is simply beyond mere mortals."

Together with Bobby Charlton, Law and Best formed a triumvirate of all-time greats who would lift United back to the very pinnacle of the sport.

CHAMPIONS OF
EUROPE AT LAST

Ten years after the Munich air disaster, Sir Matt Busby guided his side to victory in the European Cup final on an emotional night at Wembley

Words Sam Pilger

On a humid May night at Wembley, when the final whistle blew to confirm Manchester United as the first English side to win the European Cup thanks to a 4-1 victory over Benfica after extra time, the first thought of their exhausted players was to share the moment with their emotional manager Matt Busby.

By the time many of them got to him he was already surrounded by a gaggle of photographers and jubilant fans who had got on the pitch, but they waded their way through the crowd to each hug him.

"This was unquestionably the pinnacle of his football life," his captain on that night Sir Bobby Charlton has recalled. "For days he had been reminded of the meaning of the game, the legacy of Munich and how his boys had died in pursuit of this trophy. So many people believed this night was for him and about him, so it was natural everyone wanted to touch him at the end of the game."

A glowing George Best, who had scored United's crucial second goal in the final, also tightly embraced his manager. "I can still see Matt's face at the end as if it were yesterday," Best said before his death in 2005. "He wasn't crying, that came later, but he looked as if he should have had a halo over him. He had one of those faces that lights up, like the pictures you see of saints... He had achieved something which had almost cost him his life."

As his celebrating players later went on a lap of honour holding the European Cup, the football correspondent of the *Manchester Guardian* Eric Todd speculated Busby would look to the heavens seeking the approval of what he called "the spirits of Munich".

"The moment Bobby took the cup it cleansed me," said Busby. "It eased my pain of the guilt of going into Europe. It was my justification... [It was] the greatest night of my life, the fulfilment of my dearest wish to become the first English side to win the European Cup. I'm proud of the team, proud for Bobby Charlton and Billy Foulkes who have travelled the long road with me."

Busby's journey had begun in the summer of 1956 with his decision to take his young side, then the champions of England, into the European Cup for the first time. Less than two years later 23 people, including eight of his players, would die in a plane crash on a snow-covered airfield in Munich as they travelled back from a game against Red Star Belgrade.

As he lay in a German hospital bed, where he twice received the last rites, he resolved to honour the deceased by winning the European Cup.

As league champions in 1967, United were ushered back in to the European Cup for only the second time since the Munich air disaster. In this era chances to win the trophy were rare and precious, and Busby was determined to finally grasp it.

In the first round United were handed the relatively easy task of getting past the part-time Maltese champions Hibernian, who they proceeded to comfortably beat 4-0 in the first leg at Old Trafford, with two goals each from Denis Law and David Sadler, before coming through unscathed with a goalless draw on a sandy pitch in the second leg in front of an excitable crowd of 23,000 at the Empire Stadium in Gżira.

In the next round United faced the bigger test of FK Sarajevo and were relieved to come through a physical encounter with a goalless draw in the first leg in Yugoslavia.

United would take an 11th-minute lead in the second leg back at Old Trafford through John Aston before Sarajevo were reduced to ten men when their captain Fahrudin Prljača was sent off for kicking George Best. The Northern Irishman would exact his revenge by scoring a decisive second after 65 minutes, and though Sarajevo pulled a goal back United held on.

United gained a 2-0 win over Górnik Zabrze of Poland in the first leg of their quarter-final at Old Trafford, with an own goal from Stefan Florenski and a strike from Brian Kidd. It should have been more, but they were thwarted by an incredible performance from the Górnik goalkeeper Hubert Kostka.

"A Christmas card scene" is how *The Times*' Geoffrey Green described what greeted United when they arrived in southern Poland for the second leg two weeks later, but when Busby saw the snow-covered pitch he asked for the game to be postponed.

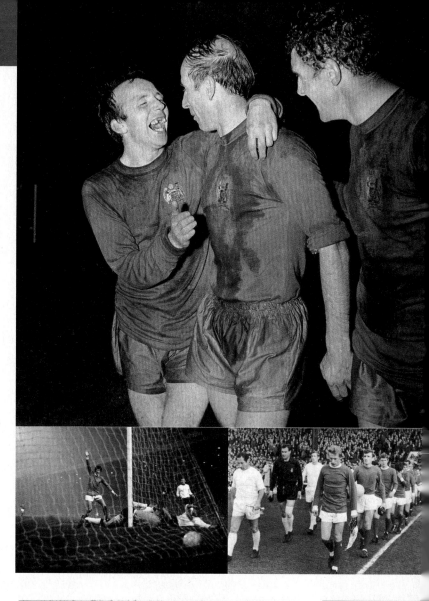

"FOR CHARLTON, THE VICTORY REPRESENTED THE COMPLETION OF A LONG AND PAINFUL JOURNEY"

The Italian referee Concetto Lo Bello dismissed this request and the game went ahead with a disciplined United determined to protect their lead, which they managed until the Poles scored 19 minutes before the end. It proved too little, too late and United went through 2-1 on aggregate. "We came to contain the foe and did the job we set out to perform," said a relieved Busby.

United were now in the semi-finals of the European Cup for the fourth time, and standing in their way of making it to the final for the first time was Real Madrid, who had already lifted the trophy on six occasions.

United secured a 1-0 win in the first leg at Old Trafford with a goal from George Best to set up a mammoth game at the Bernabéu in Madrid three weeks later (see page 25). "If we can survive there, we have a good chance in the final," said Busby. And so they did.

Awaiting United in the final at Wembley were the formidable Portuguese champions Benfica, who had won the competition in 1961 and 1962, and boasted the great Eusébio, the leading scorer in that season's competition.

But a sense of destiny emboldened United. "I just couldn't see us losing a European Cup final against Benfica at Wembley... I can remember thinking that we had come too far and been through too much to fail," said Charlton.

But the United captain also acknowledged such certainty was "a dangerous feeling", and they would need to be at their very best in

Top Nobby Stiles, Bobby Charlton and Bill Foulkes celebrate winning the European Cup on a lap of honour of Wembley
Above left George Best scores against FK Sarajevo in the second round of the European Cup
Above right Denis Law leads United out before the first leg of their semi-final against Real Madrid at Old Trafford

A DRAMATIC NIGHT IN MADRID

Manchester United reached their first-ever European Cup final by coming from behind to draw against the mighty Real Madrid

Being so close to reaching their first-ever final appeared to overwhelm United and by half-time they found themselves trailing 3-1 in the second leg of their semi-final.

The Spanish side had been majestic and completely dominated United with goals from Pirri, Gento and Armancio. "Real had been running past us as if we didn't exist," admitted John Aston.

"Anyone would have thought it was all over [at half-time], but Matt wasn't giving up that easily," Best has recalled. "On that night he showed he was one of the greats. He sprung his master plan on us by saying, 'Let's give them something to think about in the second half. He pointed at David Sadler. 'David, you move up front.'"

United were a different team after the interval but had to wait until 15 minutes

before the end to score when Sadler, acting on these instructions, stole in to the area and poked a shot past the Madrid keeper Antonio Betancort to make the tie 3-3 on aggregate.

Three minutes later it was the turn of central defender Bill Foulkes to become United's unlikely hero when he strode forward to join an attack. "Where the hell are you going?" shouted Nobby Stiles, as the United bench also told him to stay back. Foulkes did not listen to them but instead was there to tap in a cross from Best to win the tie.

Afterwards, inside a jubilant United dressing room, Busby and Charlton were both in tears. Later Busby would collect himself enough to say, "We are on the last rung of the staircase to the sky."

---

the final, which was goalless at half-time after both teams, seemingly gripped with tension, cancelled each other out.

"We were a bit down at half-time," Best has recalled. "We hadn't played near our best, but Matt told us, 'Let's keep playing it around and get at them a bit more. Let's frighten them.'"

It took only seven minutes for United to take the lead when Bobby Charlton met David Sadler's cross with a looping header that evaded the Benfica keeper José Henrique.

United protected their lead until ten minutes from the end when Jaime Graça scored with a low shot across Alex Stepney, and soon after, Benfica had the chance to win the game when Eusébio found himself free and advanced on United's goal.

"I was horrified to see Eusébio bearing down on us," Charlton has recalled. But Stepney came out to narrow the angle and Eusébio opted to beat him with power instead of placement, with a shot the United keeper managed to hold on to. "It thudded into my chest," Stepney has said. "We played with a Mitre ball and I said the make of the ball was imprinted backwards on my shirt! I admit it did hurt me."

Minutes later the referee blew for the end of normal time and United's exhausted players sat on the Wembley turf as Busby spoke

Below Pat Crerand, Matt Busby and George Best hold the European Cup during their celebrations at a London hotel after the final

to them. "They're getting tired, they're not used to this pitch," he said pointing to the Benfica players. "Let's go back to what we were doing before. Let's keep the ball and make them do all the running."

Two minutes in to extra time a long clearance from Stepney was flicked on by Brian Kidd to Best, who beat Fernando Cruz before going around the keeper and knocking the ball into an empty net to give United a lead they would not lose.

The goal would deflate the Portuguese and inspire United, who scored twice more in the next seven minutes with a header from Brian Kidd on his 19th birthday and another expertly taken goal from Charlton.

For Charlton, the victory represented the completion of a long and painful journey that had driven him and his manager for ten years.

"At the final whistle, I felt more relief than joy," Charlton once told me. "I was so very, very tired. It was an emotional night. We had won it for Matt Busby and all the boys who should have been there. The one thing I remember is how heavy the European Cup was when I lifted it, I nearly dropped it. But despite the tiredness, I think it was the best I had ever felt after a match, even better than winning the World Cup, as for me it was more important."

UNITED THEY FALL

Manchester United went from European champions to relegation
to the Second Division in the space of just six years

Words Sam Pilger

On the morning after winning the 1968 European Cup Final, George Best was arguably the best footballer in the world. He had just been voted the Footballer of the Year; he would soon become the youngest-ever winner of the Ballon d'Or, and his 28 goals from the previous season were the main inspiration behind United becoming European champions.

It should have been the start of a glorious new era for both him and United, but it soon proved to be the beginning of the end, and within six years United had completed their fall from grace by being relegated to the Second Division.

"I think quite a few players thought we had done what we set out to do and relaxed a bit... you could almost hear the energy and ambition sighing out of the club," Best has recalled. "The willingness to win didn't completely disappear, but it didn't seem quite so important now. It was like being at the winding up of a company."

United's manager Sir Matt Busby was now old, tired and largely sated and had remained for one more season to try to successfully defend his European title, but United would ultimately be knocked out in the semi-finals by AC Milan.

In the summer of 1969, after 24 years as manager, Busby stood down and was replaced by 31-year-old Wilf McGuinness, a former United player who had been forced to retire aged only 22 before becoming a coach at the club and also with England. He had, however, never before managed a club.

It appeared an uninspiring choice that failed to grasp the mammoth job McGuinness had in front of him; taking charge of a

Above United legend Denis Law scores for rivals City, relegating United to the Second Division

group of ageing, unmotivated players, many of whom were not supportive of him.

"I don't know who was more surprised, the players or Wilf," Best has said. "I liked him... But taking over the first team was a task he was never going to win and one of his first problems was that, at the age of 32, he was younger than some of the players. That would make it hard for him to win their respect."

Charlton believed McGuinness had been placed in "an impossible situation", and so it proved as he proceeded to win only one of his first eight league games. United might have reached the FA Cup and League Cup semi-finals, but a final finish of eighth in the First Division was deemed a failure.

The club persevered with McGuinness for the following season, but by December 1970 fears of getting dragged into a relegation battle were starting to creep in with United sitting 18th in table and having also been beaten in the League Cup semi-finals by Third Division Aston Villa.

The United board decided to sack McGuinness, with Busby later admitting, "He might have been a wee bit raw." Busby was asked to return as a caretaker manager to oversee the rest of the campaign.

At the end of that season, Busby stepped aside for a second and final time to make way for the Leicester City manager Frank O'Farrell. Busby described O'Farrell's arrival at Old Trafford as "my last great signing, possibly the greatest of the lot," amid renewed grumbling from United players that once again they had hoped for a more ambitious appointment.

"DOCHERTY DISPENSED WITH THE LEGENDARY TRIO OF BEST, CHARLTON AND LAW, WHO ALL LEFT UNITED WITHIN A YEAR OF HIS ARRIVAL"

Above left United won promotion after a season in the Second Division **Left** Best in 1971, when United's glory days were far behind them **Right** Frank O'Farrell endured an unsuccessful spell at United **Below** United's Steve Coppell during the 1976 FA Cup Final **Bottom** Busby with Wilf McGuinness

By Christmas 1971 it appeared that Busby had got it right this time, with United holding a five-point lead at the top of the First Division, but this would prove the high point of O'Farrell's reign and United would lose 11 of their last 19 league games in the new year to fall back to a final position of eighth.

Despite this the United board still backed O'Farrell in the transfer market, with the purchases of Martin Buchan and Ian Storey-Moore, and later Ted MacDougall and Wyn Davies, but they could do little to unite an increasingly fractious dressing room, undermined by the now erratic Best, who at one stage even announced his premature retirement at the age of 26.

"We'd beaten Real Madrid and Benfica, and now the Coventrys and Stokes were stuffing us at home, it was painful," Best had said.

O'Farrell (who sadly passed away on 7 March 2022) continued to limp on until a 5-0 defeat to Crystal Palace at Selhurst Park in December 1972 forced United to sack him. "[He] came as a stranger and left as a stranger," observed an unimpressed Denis Law.

Six days later the Scotland manager Tommy Docherty, who had previously taken charge of Chelsea and Aston Villa, became United's fourth manager in the last two seasons.

"The club was in turmoil," Docherty has said. "I'd inherited the remnants of the 1968 European Cup-winning team. Many had been great players, but they were past their sell-by date."

Docherty dispensed with the legendary trio of Best, Charlton and Law, who all left the club within a year of his arrival, followed by as many as 29 other players as the club was completely overhauled and remodelled into a leaner and younger side.

But progress was slow, and although Docherty staved off relegation in 1973, finishing just five points from safety, a year later he could not prevent United dropping into the Second Division. Their demotion was confirmed on a traumatic day at Old Trafford in April 1974 with a 1-0 loss to Manchester City, courtesy of a back-heeled goal from none other than Law.

Despite playing outside the top flight for the first time since 1938, United held their nerve and stood by Docherty, who they believed would quickly be able to get results with his squad of talented younger players, including Stuart Pearson, Gerry Daly, Sammy McIlroy and Lou Macari.

They were proved right as United won the Second Division championship with a series of exciting performances in front of full crowds at Old Trafford.

"Don't expect too much too soon," declared Docherty during the summer of 1975 on their return to the First Division after just one season away, but his young side surprised even him by finishing third, just four points behind the champions Liverpool, and also reaching the FA Cup Final for the first time in 13 years only to lose 1-0 to Southampton at Wembley. They'd go one better two years later.

FROM THE FFT ARCHIVES:
JUNE 2017

"AND THE BEST THING BOYS...
WE STOPPED LIVERPOOL
DOING THE TREBLE"

All-conquering Liverpool went into the 1977 FA Cup Final
eyeing a then-unprecedented treble, and only one team
could stop them making history: Manchester United

Words Leo Moynihan

Image Alamy Images

"I was looking forward to it," said Manchester United manager Tommy Docherty following his fourth FA Cup final appearance as a player or manager. "But I thought, 'Liverpool have won the Championship, they're going for the treble and have got the European Cup final the Wednesday after the cup final'. I wasn't too confident, I must say."

Two things stand out about this statement from the man they called 'The Doc'. Firstly, it's lacking the sheer Glaswegian brass-ballsiness that the game grew to expect from him over the years. Where is his cavalier approach that so epitomised the man and his dynamic football teams?

Secondly, his cautious words totally belie the mood that he, as the manager of Manchester United, set on the morning of the FA Cup final 40 years ago. From the start of that sunny day, as the country dug in for eight hours in front of the television, Docherty set a comical and uber-relaxed tone from their hotel, despite pundits talking mainly of Bob Paisley and Liverpool making history.

He had his morning shave, teased midfielder Lou Macari over breakfast for being teetotal, and stepped outside for a game of croquet on the hotel's front lawn with comedian Ronnie Corbett – all of this going on in front of the watching television cameras.

"Now, don't run through the croquet hoop," Tommy quipped to the pint-sized co-king of Saturday night TV. Yes, on the morning of the FA Cup final, Docherty did not seem to possess a smidgen of self-doubt. If this was sheer bravado though, then who could blame him? His United team, as exciting as they may have been, were hours away from facing Liverpool, the new force in European football. The Reds had already retained the league title (the first team to do so since Wolves in '59), had won the UEFA Cup the season before and were straight off to Rome after this Wembley clash for the European Cup final against Borussia Monchengladbach.

Docherty's side were good but, away from the cameras, he must have dwelt on his label as "the most successful failure in football" – cruelly stuck to his lapel due to his hitherto inability to taste victory at the Twin Towers. As a player he'd lost there with Preston in '54 and with Scotland in '55, '57 and '59. And as a manager he'd lost in cup finals with Chelsea in '67 and with United in '76. And then you had Bob Paisley, who in terms of character was his total antithesis. There would be less joviality in front of the cameras, but surely the quiet man from Durham would have no such doubts?

Since taking over from Bill Shankly, Paisley had taken a great side and, with subtle tweaks, made it even greater.

Liverpool's ability to seamlessly adjust to losing a legend like Shankly in '74 was in stark contrast to their rivals, who'd struggled so much to cope post-Matt Busby that talk of ghosts around Old Trafford seemed more than mere metaphor. Docherty had taken the reins in '72, but his ageing squad were relegated two years later. It was then that he set about building a new, younger team.

"The Doc built a side defined by width," right-winger Steve Coppell tells *FourFourTwo*. "He had played at Preston with Tom Finney and idolised him, and our game was about getting it out wide. Attack, attack, attack." Fans came in their droves.

"For me," says Gary Thompson, a United fan and teenager in the 1970s, "other than the treble season in 1998-99, the year we spent in the second division was my favourite." With flair and excitement, United bounced straight back and their team became a byword for entertainment. Docherty had them challenging Liverpool and QPR for the 1975-76 title before settling for an FA Cup final, but then the Wembley jinx hit with second-tier Southampton the shock winners. "That was devastating," remembers Lou Macari. "The next day, we still had this open-top bus ride and thousands of fans came out. The Doc grabbed the microphone and said we'd be back in a year with the cup. The crowd cheered, but us players looked at each other and thought, 'This guy's mad'."

At Liverpool, results did all the talking as the 1976-77 campaign rumbled on. Since overcoming a brilliant Saint-Etienne side in the

Above Paisley and Docherty lead their charges out at Wembley
Right United's Stuart Pearson competes with Joey Jones for aerial supremacy
Below "It's fun to stay at the..."

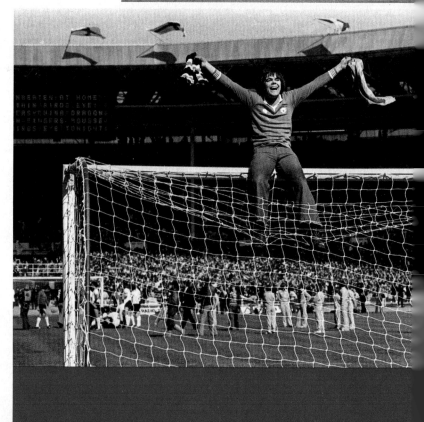

European Cup quarter-finals, and Everton in the FA Cup semi-finals, word 'treble' was on the country's eager lips. Everywhere except Anfield, of course. "No, there was none of that," says left-back Joey Jones. "Bob and his staff wouldn't have any of that and nor would us players. We simply didn't talk about it."

However, Peter Etherington, a Liverpool fan in his early 20s at the time, was having none of the club's caution. "You started to hear it on the Kop and after Saint-Etienne it got even louder. 'We're gonna win the treble!' We just felt unbeatable."

Liverpool, steered by Paisley and his backroom staff, were a squad focused on winning silverware. "They were incredibly professional," explains Coppell. "They would socialise loads, but as soon as they crossed that white line, something clicked. No team was more on it." The country's back pages might have been screaming 'TREBLE' but at the Reds' Melwood training base the staff trusted their players to stay calm and look after themselves, mentally and physically. Once, esteemed full-back Phil Neal went to coach Joe Fagan with concerns. "Joe, on Saturday, should I be showing the winger inside or outside?" "You tell me," Fagan deadpanned in reply to the defender. "You're the one who f**king plays for England."

"THE DOC TOLD THE FANS WE WOULD BE BACK IN A YEAR WITH THE CUP. THE CROWD CHEERED BUT US PLAYERS THOUGHT, 'THIS GUY'S MAD'"

Below Respectful rivals in the 1970s, Wembley was awash with red-and-white flags and scarves

Simple but forward-thinking, Liverpool circa '77 won the title with a game to spare after a 0-0 draw against West Ham. Unlike the year before when they had nicked it with late goals at Wolves – sparking mass celebrations up the M6 – this was a far more subdued affair.

"It was almost as though the fans had taken a title triumph for granted and they were preoccupied with the FA Cup final that was coming up," admitted Paisley at the time. "Even inside our dressing room there was no champagne. Everyone sensed that winning the league title was just the first of a three-round contest – that puts into perspective the position we've reached."

That position was still some way from the summit they hoped to scale, though. So without wanting to complicate things, Paisley had to decide on team selection for two finals in five days. Rotation was an alien concept back then. Emlyn Hughes would play 62 games in 1976-77, but outside factors had got into the gaffer's head and his decisions would be unusually compromised.

The FA had announced that due to the Merseysiders' European commitments, any potential FA Cup final replay would be played on 27 June, during the Wimbledon tennis championships and just a fortnight before pre-season training began.

Paisley and Docherty were both incensed. "We'll have to take our holidays on the Costa del Stretford," joked the latter. Paisley called for a penalty shootout but the FA's decision was final. In response, Paisley picked a team to win the game, opting for a more attacking 4-3-3 and dropping the more pragmatic Ian Callaghan to the bench.

● ● ● ●

So, off both teams went to north London, followed vociferously and colourfully by their frantic supporters, for a clash that today would be tinged with vitriolic nastiness. "Back then, there was not the same hatred as now," says United fan, Gary Thompson. "In fact, you

could say it was the last encounter between the two that wasn't really bad in terms of trouble. The two semi-finals in '79 were bad, and the '83 League Cup Final went down in folklore for its trouble, but I don't recall anything too bad in '77."

Fans arrived, their flared trousers covering their Doc Marten boots, Wrangler jackets, feather-cut hairstyles and scarves around their wrists. Not that it was all fashion and mutual respect. "Trouble was part of football back then," says Dave Kirby, an 18-year-old Liverpool fan at the time. "We arrived in a minibus at 6.30 a.m. and ran into this group of Mancs. We got into a bit of a battle with them and suddenly this bottle was flying towards my head.

"I was off to Rome on the Monday so I got a new tattoo with the Liverpool crest on my arm. At Wembley I put out my hand to stop the bottle and it smashed. Blood everywhere. I went to hospital for stitches and still have the scar today. I got the tattoo from a needle prick, and the scar from a Manc prick!"

Another man with his own problems was a young John Motson, a jobbing commentator with the BBC now entrusted with his first showpiece occasion. "David Coleman had some sort of contractual dispute with the bosses," he recalls. "That meant the final was up for grabs and I got it over Barry Davies. I was so nervous. The cup final was the live game and my first live broadcast – I was worried I would make some sort of faux pas."

For both sets of players, there was no such worry. Liverpool were Liverpool and United arrived on Wembley Way unshackled by the pressures they felt a year earlier. "I remember being relaxed," says Macari. "This time, while we were hugely motivated, the favourites tag wasn't with us and we felt good."

Coppell agrees. "You have to remember that Liverpool were seen as an express train and we were next in line to be rolled over. We'd been there the year before, though. We knew what to expect, were

Below United celebrate Pearson's opening goal

well prepared and motivated not to feel the despair that we had felt against Southampton. I grew up a Liverpool fan. My brother went to Rome a few days later, but there were no mixed feelings. I wasn't going through what I went through in '76."

Liverpool, so used to the burden of being the favourites, wouldn't be hindered by it. "I had only made my debut two years before but it soon became clear you had to deal with pressure to play for the club," says midfielder Jimmy Case. "Being good wasn't enough. You had to have something above the neck. I remember Ray Kennedy, who I roomed with for years, sitting up in bed, mentioning all of the massive games we'd played in. 'Is this normal?' he said. It felt like it was, but looking back, I guess it wasn't."

The match itself was a cagey affair, one that only burst into life in a five-minute spell early in the second period. Stuart Pearson gave United the lead before John Motson put his professional worries to one side when he astutely said, "There is a saying in football that Liverpool are at their most dangerous when behind." On cue, Joey Jones lofted the ball up to Case ("I was aiming for Keegan!") who controlled it on his thigh, swivelled and fired beyond Alex Stepney.

"PAISLEY SAT IN HIS LIVING ROOM, POURED HIMSELF A SCOTCH AND WROTE DOWN THE STARTING XI FOR THE EUROPEAN CUP FINAL"

Minutes later, United's winner was as messy as Case's goal was brilliant. Macari darted into the box, the ball bounced around and he took aim. "I screamed at Jimmy [Greenhoff] to get out the way. The ball lofted over [Ray] Clemence and we were winning."

Cue mayhem in the United end and the commentary box. "Macari is it?" asked Motson, brilliantly – but unwittingly – summing up all of the confusion. It had actually struck the chest of Greenhoff to take it in and only eagle-eyed co-commentator Jimmy Hill had noticed. "Jimmy nudged me and said Greenhoff, but the action replay was from the same angle so it was hard to tell for a while," says Motson. Despite waves of Liverpool pressure, the Red Devils held firm and the cup was won.

"For the remainder of the game, and as I went up the steps to get my medal, I thought that I had scored the winner," laughs Macari. "Back then they gave a golden boot to the scorer of the winning goal and even when I saw Jimmy with it in the tunnel I didn't realise. Eventually I was informed but it wasn't important. We'd won and that's all that really mattered."

● ● ● ●

That evening both sets of players ended up throwing things at each other. United threw a banquet in a hotel off Park Lane and manager, players and friends ended up on Hyde Park. "It was late at night and we all went out and were tossing the cup between us," says Macari. "I think it ended up with quite a few dents in it."

For Liverpool, the treble dream was now over. They had dejectedly lapped the Wembley pitch amid cheers (and even some sporting applause from United's jubilant faithful) before setting off to catch their train home.

Suddenly, Clemence stood up and declared that he was going to get drunk, and just a few glasses of wine later, the team and their wives were throwing sugar cubes at each other in scenes unbefitting of the sombre situation. "That was Steve Heighway," laughs Case. "He went to university, had all the brains in the world, but no common sense."

Hours later, the train carriage a mess and their heads a little bleary, the team were home with the defeat, like London, well behind them. Paisley sat in his living room, poured himself a Scotch and then wrote down the starting XI for the European Cup final.

This time Callaghan played from the start and this time the game was won, Liverpool defeating Gladbach 3-1. Denied a treble but still victorious, Paisley basked in the glory that was Rome.

Tommy Docherty took the cup he had promised back to Manchester, but then just as his stock was highest, he was fired for having an affair with the club physio's wife Mary, to whom he is still married. It was an unfortunate and perhaps harsh conclusion to an incredibly entertaining tenure. "I'm the only manager ever to be sacked for falling in love," he later said. Lou Macari can only smile upon hearing the line. "That's typical of The Doc – never short of something to say."

Clockwise from above
Pearson takes aim and lashes United ahead; Docherty celebrates after finally ending his Wembley hoodoo; United parade their unexpected trophy; The Liverpool players acknowledge their fans

THAT'S ENTERTAINMENT

Ron Atkinson brought the fun and the flair back to Manchester United,
and a couple of FA Cups too, but he just fell short in the league

Words Rob Clark

On the face of it, Ron Atkinson should have been the perfect fit for Manchester United – a larger-than-life character with bags of personality who wasn't fazed by managing star players, knew how to work the media and wanted his team to play with flair. 'Big Ron' was also the perfect antidote to the somewhat dour Dave Sexton, who had never been popular with United's fans due to his safety-first approach.

Sexton had lasted four years but had failed to land a trophy (losing 3-2 to Arsenal in the dramatic 1979 FA Cup Final and finishing as runners-up to Liverpool the following season were the closest he got). Sexton actually did decent business in the transfer market, freshening up the side with the signings of Gary Bailey and Kevin Moran, plus the Leeds United duo of Joe Jordan and Gordon McQueen, giving United greater physical presence at both front and back. The capture of McQueen was accompanied by one of the great football quotes of all time, when the big Scotsman declared, "Ask all the players in the country which club they would like to join and 99 per cent would say 'Manchester United'. The other one per cent would be liars."

But the club decided that the pizzazz was missing, and Atkinson certainly brought that. Moving from West Bromwich Albion, who that season finished above United in the league, he insisted on bringing Bryan Robson and Remi Moses with him. With typical Atkinson flair, Robson was signed on the pitch before the match against Wolverhampton Wanderers on 3 October 1981. There were doubts about the 24 year old who had already experienced injury problems, but Atkinson was determined. "This one ain't a gamble," he told Chairman Martin Edwards. "He's solid gold." And so he was. Captain Marvel was a born winner and worthy of a place in central midfield in any club side in any era in history.

During his five-year reign, Atkinson's United finished third twice and fourth three times. They also won the FA Cup twice in three years, a trophy that somehow seemed to suit the flamboyance of the manager better than the day in, day out slog of the league.

Certainly, Atkinson's team could swagger with the best of them when the mood took them. In 1983 they beat Luton Town, West Ham, Everton and Arsenal – all Division One teams – plus Derby County to reach the final, conceding just one goal, against Arsenal in the semi-final. Brighton & Hove Albion were the underdogs in the final, but it's too easily forgotten that they too were a top-flight side at the time and had beaten Liverpool at Anfield in a previous round. Maybe underestimating their opponents almost cost United dear, and in extra time Gordon Smith, who had put Brighton ahead way back in the 14th minute, had a one-on-one with Gary Bailey to win the cup. Radio commentator Peter Jones coined the now famous "and Smith must score" quote, but Smith's miss meant there would be a replay the following week.

Above right A relaxed-looking Atkinson with the FA Cup after the 1983 final replay
Right United celebrate victory over Everton in the 1985 FA Cup Final
Below Atkinson and Alex Ferguson lead out their trophy-laden United and Aberdeen teams for Martin Buchan's testimonial in 1983

Bottom
Atkinson enjoys a glass of champagne in his office
Below right
Bryan Robson signs for United watched by (left to right) Ron Atkinson, Secretary Les Olive and Chairman Martin Edwards

We must note in passing that Bailey, a fine goalkeeper, always felt Smith was rather hard done by. "It wasn't a miss," he said pointedly. "Gordon's shot was on target. It was a save."

Five days later it was an altogether more ruthless United that took the field. Three first-half goals killed the game and a penalty on the hour made it 4-0. It was the sort of pacy, powerful football that Atkinson had been brought to the club to instil.

Two seasons later, they did it again. The final could not have been against tougher opponents – a Howard Kendall-managed Everton side who were not only the holders of the trophy, but who won the league and European Cup Winners' Cup that year and had already beaten United twice: a 5-0 shellacking at Goodison and a 2-1 League Cup victory at Old Trafford. An even – and frankly somewhat unexciting – game was shaken into life in the 78th minute when Kevin Moran was shown a harsh red card for bringing down the Toffees' dynamic midfielder, Peter Reid. It was the first FA Cup Final sending-off, but if anything it seemed to spur United on. The match was decided by a single goal, but what a strike it was, Norman Whiteside cutting in from the right wing and hitting an unstoppable curling left-foot shot past the great Neville Southall.

The 1985–86 season started with a run of ten straight wins, but United's form fell away and they finished a distant fourth. With the pressure building at the start of the 1986–87 season and performances still patchy, Atkinson was dismissed. In classic Atkinson style, he threw the players a party to say goodbye. As for his time in charge, Atkinson once declared, "Managing Manchester United? Hey, that will do for me."

"IT WAS THE SORT OF PACY, POWERFUL FOOTBALL THAT ATKINSON HAD BEEN BROUGHT TO THE CLUB TO INSTIL"

Images Getty Images

THE MAN FROM
ABERDEEN

When Manchester United decided in 1986 to find a new man to fill the dugout,
their was only one manager they had in mind: a fiery young Scot named Alex
Ferguson. But would he survive long enough to make an impact?

Words Sam Pilger

n the wake of Ron Atkinson's departure in 1986 Manchester United were only ever interested in one manager to succeed him: Alex Ferguson.

Over the previous two decades United had often failed to secure their first choice candidate for the dugout and had been forced to compromise, but in the autumn of 1986 they were determined to draw Ferguson away from Aberdeen to become their new manager.

At Pittodrie, Ferguson had spectacularly broken the Glaswegian monopoly of Scottish football, winning three Scottish titles, four Scottish Cups, one Scottish League Cup and the European Cup Winners' Cup in 1983 after beating Real Madrid in the final.

"My thinking was: If he can do that at Aberdeen, what can he achieve at Manchester United?" said the club's chairman Martin Edwards. "He was young and ambitious and had a reputation for being a strong manager. You could see his fire and enthusiasm."

Ferguson had already turned down approaches from Rangers, Arsenal and Tottenham, but he could not resist the allure of United when they made contact and met him on Guy Fawkes Day in 1986.

"When the opportunity came to join Manchester United I could no longer stay in my safe house in Aberdeen," Ferguson has said. "I felt I had not achieved enough, and once you stop striving in football it's time to chuck it all in, and so I was ready."

Ferguson walked in to a struggling club stranded in the relegation zone and already out of the League Cup after an embarrassing 4-1 defeat to Southampton in the third round. He also had to contend with a disjointed squad of players, with too many of them not fit enough, not committed enough, or simply not good enough.

Right United chairman Martin Edwards and Alex Ferguson announce the signings of Viv Anderson and Brian McClair in July 1987

Ferguson started his squad rebuild, moving on seven players and entering the transfer market in the summer of 1987 with gusto; he might have failed to sign Peter Beardsley and John Barnes, who both went to Liverpool, but he did manage to bring in the Arsenal defender Viv Anderson and the Celtic striker Brian McClair, before adding Steve Bruce from Norwich City in December that year.

In the 1987–88 season a more confident Ferguson, helped by these new players, lifted United to a second-placed finish, their highest since 1980, but at no point were they ever in a meaningful title race with Liverpool, who finished a comfortable nine points ahead of them.

That summer Ferguson brought Mark Hughes back to the club from Barcelona and purchased his old goalkeeper Jim Leighton from Aberdeen, but any progress from the previous season was lost as United tumbled back to an embarrassing finish of 11th.

Ferguson still did not fully trust many of the players in his dressing room. "I resolved that I had to change everything round and gather a squad around me capable of winning the league. I just knew I had to go for it," he has said.

Arsenal had won the league title in 1989 to break seven years of Merseyside dominance to further inspire Ferguson. "[Arsenal manager] George Graham had challenged the might of Anfield and come out on top, which gave me the impetus I needed. I resolved there and then that if he could do it so could I."

In the summer of 1989 Ferguson spent £7.5 million on five players – Gary Pallister, Mike Phelan, Danny Wallace, Neil Webb and Paul Ince – while allowing three major players – Norman Whiteside, Paul McGrath and Gordon Strachan – to leave for new clubs.

On the opening day of the season Old Trafford glowed with optimism after United defeated the champions Arsenal 4-1. New signing Neil Webb, who had scored a stunning goal, later recalled, "After we had completely outplayed them I walked off the pitch with the crowd giving us a great reception, thinking, 'The changes really seemed to have worked. This could be a big year for us'. It was to be a terrible false dawn."

Webb would soon pick up an injury that ruled him out for seven months, and the other new signings struggled as United lost three of their next four league games before being humiliated 5-1 by Manchester City at Maine Road at the end of September.

"Every time somebody looks at me I feel as if I have betrayed that man," Ferguson told *The Sunday Times* about his state of mind in the week following the loss to City. "After such a result you feel you have to creep around corners, feel as if you are some kind of criminal. But that's only because you care deeply."

Ferguson wasn't being melodramatic or exaggerating how unpopular he had become, as both United's fans and players were rapidly losing faith.

He had been given time and money, but it wasn't working, and during the winter of 1989 United went on a painful run of 11 league games without a win that saw them slump to 17th in the table.

During a 2-1 defeat to Crystal Palace at an agitated Old Trafford hosting 14,000 fewer fans than on that sun-bathed opening day, chants of "Fergie out" could be heard on the cold air, and the man himself recalls being "howled out of the ground". That same day one supporter, Peter Molyneux, famously unfurled a banner in the stands with the message, "Three years of excuses. Ta-ra Fergie."

After a crucial FA Cup win over Nottingham Forest (see page 41), United's form in the First Division continued to fluctuate, and it wasn't until April that they finally pulled themselves clear of the relegation zone, but in the FA Cup they were able to beat Hereford, Newcastle, Sheffield United and Oldham (after a replay) to reach the final against Crystal Palace.

In a classic Wembley final United and Palace swapped the lead three times during 120 frantic minutes; the Londoners went 1-0 in front in the first half before goals from Robson and Hughes gave United a 2-1 lead, only for Ian Wright to come on as a substitute and score twice. Hughes rescued United by scoring with seven minutes of extra time left to end the game 3-3 and ensure a replay.

"FERGUSON HAD ALREADY TURNED DOWN APPROACHES FROM RANGERS, ARSENAL AND TOTTENHAM, BUT COULD NOT RESIST THE ALLURE OF UNITED"

Left Alex Ferguson greets the fans before his first game as United manager at Old Trafford in November 1986

Ferguson would lose his first game in charge, 2-0 away to Oxford United, a game that left him shocked at his players' overall quality, particularly their physicality and fitness.

"I came to the conclusion the players' standard of fitness was simply not good enough," Ferguson has said. "There was no way they were able to compete in 60 battles over a season."

Ferguson introduced a new training regime, with longer and tougher sessions overseen by his trusted assistant, Archie Knox, who he had brought with him from Aberdeen, which the United captain Bryan Robson quickly claimed made him feel stronger than ever.

This helped inspire United to a run of only two defeats in 16 league games between November and March, an upturn in form that lifted them clear of the relegation zone to a final finish of 11th, which was still their lowest top-flight finish since they were relegated in 1974.

Ferguson was brave enough to admit he had realised he had "no real inkling about the demands... and no manager [could be] prepared for the job at Old Trafford. For the first time in my life I felt my whole character and abilities were under scrutiny."

"When I met the directors at the end of my first half season I told them we needed nine new players to win the championship. To put it mildly, I think they were surprised. We had too many players the wrong side of 28, who were too old to go for the challenges I had in mind... they had lost the magic spark."

Images Getty Images

Five days later United lined up at Wembley with the same side except for one crucial difference; Jim Leighton, who had been culpable for two of Palace's goals in the first game, had been dropped by Ferguson for his back-up goalkeeper Les Sealey, who was on loan from Luton and had only played twice for United that season.

The replay offered significantly less drama than the final, with both sides less willing to pour forward. It was settled 1-0 after exactly an hour when Webb found Lee Martin's surging run from the back with a brilliant pass before he smashed his shot past Nigel Martyn.

"I will always remember the relief on Ferguson's face and among all the players as we travelled back on the train to Manchester with the FA Cup as company," Webb remembered later. "There was a feeling that we had survived the dark days and this club could enjoy a lot of success again."

Initially this would not manifest itself in the league; after only signing Denis Irwin in the summer, United made good progress to finish sixth in the table, but again it was in the cup competitions where United performed best.

While United's defence of the FA Cup would end in the fifth round with defeat to Norwich City, in the League Cup highly impressive victories over champions Liverpool and Arsenal in the earlier rounds would see them face Sheffield Wednesday in the final at Wembley.

Top left Mark Hughes attempts a spectacular volley against Tottenham at White Hart Lane in October 1988
Top right United line up before the 1991 European Cup Winners' Cup against Barcelona in Rotterdam
Above Manchester United celebrate winning the FA Cup in May 1990
Left Mark Hughes with the 1991 European Cup Winners' Cup trophy

Wednesday, led by former United manager Ron Atkinson, proved to be stubborn opposition and frustrated their favoured opponents, who could not summon up the same spirit shown at Wembley 11 months earlier and fell to a tepid 1-0 defeat. "We should have murdered Sheffield Wednesday... [but] made the fatal mistake of underestimating them," Ferguson said.

There was some consolation to be found in Europe. After UEFA had lifted their five-year ban on English clubs, United would go one step further in the European Cup Winners' Cup to claim their first European trophy for 23 years.

They had a relatively easy passage to the final, overcoming Pécsi Munkás, Wrexham, Montpellier and Legia Warsaw, but in the final in Rotterdam they faced a revered Barcelona side managed by the Dutch legend Johan Cruyff, who had just won the first of four consecutive La Liga titles that season.

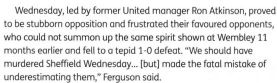

"MARK HUGHES WAS DETERMINED TO SHOW HIS FORMER CLUB WHAT THEY WERE MISSING AND PUT UNITED IN FRONT"

Mark Hughes, who had endured an unhappy two seasons at Barcelona, was determined to show his former club what they were missing and put United in front from close range in the first half. He would double United's lead in the second half with a powerful shot from what at first looked to be an impossibly tight angle.

After Ronald Koeman had pulled a goal back for Barça, United were indebted to Clayton Blackmore for blocking a Michael Laudrup shot on the line to keep United in front and deliver them Ferguson's second trophy at Old Trafford.

After these two trophies in two years, and the astute signings of Peter Schmeichel, Paul Parker and Andrei Kanchelskis during the summer, Ferguson felt confident enough to state United were ready to finally win the First Division again.

"Flushed with success in Europe, I stuck my neck right out," Ferguson has recalled. "Some no doubt considered I was foolish to be so bold, but I honestly thought we were ripe for a serious assault on the league championship. It was a declaration of intention for the supporters of United."

These bold words were backed by deeds for the first half of the season, as United, playing with great flair, raced to the top of the table after winning eight of their first ten league games. They also won the club's first European Super Cup thanks to a 1-0 win over the European champions Red Star Belgrade.

The new year of 1992 should have seen United claim their first league title for 25 years, but instead, on its very first day, United fell to an unexpected 4-1 defeat to QPR at Old Trafford that first revealed the fragile confidence that would ultimately undermine them.

United would go on to win their first-ever League Cup with a 1-0 victory over Nottingham Forest in the final at Wembley, but with so much still at stake in the league it felt like a warm-up act.

United's run to this final had seen their fixtures pile up, and after it they faced the daunting prospect of playing five league games in ten

Above Ian Rush celebrates scoring past Peter Schmeichel on the day United lost the title race at Anfield in April 1992

days to decide the title race. They started with a 1-0 win over Southampton but then drew with Luton and lost consecutive games to Forest and West Ham to allow Leeds United to overtake them.

When United took to the pitch for their penultimate game of the season against Liverpool at Anfield they knew anything less than a win would see Leeds handed the title. But United's exhausted players would run out of steam at the worst time, and at the worst venue imaginable, to lose 2-0 to Liverpool, whose fans relished every moment and unfurled a gloating banner that read, "Have you ever seen United win the league?"

"Missing out on the title hurt," the side's captain Bryan Robson has said. "I'd been close to the title a few times, but this was the worst feeling because there is no doubt we should have won it... We lost three of our last four games as we were simply dead on our feet."

FERGUSON'S TURNING POINT

A crucial FA Cup win over Nottingham Forest saved Ferguson's job and helped him win his first trophy as United manager

As United continued to lurk around the bottom of the table during the winter of 1989, it became perceived wisdom that if they lost their FA Cup third-round tie to Nottingham Forest then Alex Ferguson's three-year reign as manager would be ended.

"Ferguson's transfer policy has been a disaster, his team selection has often made little sense and results, given the greatness of the club, have been abysmal. Today his job literally hangs in the balance," wrote Brian Glanville in *The Sunday Times*.

On 7 January 1990, United, who were missing several important players through injury, went into the game at the City Ground as firm underdogs against cup specialists Forest. "Everyone was smelling defeat for us," Ferguson later said.

However, a resilient United managed to eke out a 1-0 win thanks to a headed goal from their young striker Mark Robins after important build-up work from Lee Martin and Mark Hughes.

"I think we did it that day with defiance from the supporters, and the players responded to their promptings," Ferguson has said. "Right from the word go they were on song our support. They were not going to lose that game."

Images Getty Images

THE CLASS OF '92

It isn't often a youth team has a documentary dedicated to it, but then it isn't often that youth team football produces the sort of players United did in the early 1990s

Words Rob Clark

You can't win anything with kids!" Alan Hansen's damning verdict on Manchester United's chances with a young side has passed into folklore as a terrible prediction. But in fact Alex Ferguson agreed with the sentiment in general terms. What he knew, and Hansen did not, is that 'his' kids were an exception to the rule – a once-in-a-lifetime exception. The most talented group of youngsters since the Busby Babes, Ferguson's Fledglings were all set to take the Premiership by storm and at the end of the 1995–96 season (at the start of which Hansen had made his faux pas) United had won a league and cup double.

Amid all the numerous comings and goings of players and coaches during Ron Atkinson's time in charge, one name that was overlooked at the time was Eric Harrison. Lured from Everton to be youth-team coach, Harrison was the driving force behind the youth policy at the club, a policy that had the firm backing of Alex Ferguson.

The United 'method' was based around getting youth-team players ready for first-team football. To this end, they ensured that they had the same system in place throughout the club, whatever the age group. They also abandoned the traditional eight-a-side matches in favour of four-a-side games that allowed young players to work on their technique and not worry about results.

The players who became known as the Class of '92 won the FA Youth Cup that year, beating Crystal Palace 3-1 in the first leg and 3-2 in the second with a team that included Ryan Giggs, David Beckham, Nicky Butt and Gary Neville. Several of the players who did not become household names – including Chris Casper and Ben Thornley – were held back by serious injuries, while Robbie Savage and Colin McKee found success elsewhere. Paul Scholes and Phil Neville didn't feature until the following year, but nevertheless became associated with the now legendary Class of '92.

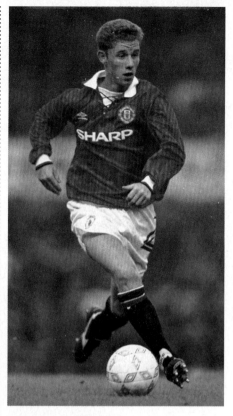

RYAN GIGGS

BIRTH DATE: **29 NOVEMBER 1973**
DEBUT: **2 MARCH 1991 (VS EVERTON)**

Strictly speaking, Ryan Giggs wasn't part of the Class of '92; he had made his first-team debut in March 1991, and his first start a couple of months later. That came against rivals Manchester City on 4 May, and Giggs got the only goal of the game. In reality, his shot took a huge deflection off City's Scottish defender Colin Hendry, but as Giggs said, at 17 he wasn't going to argue with being credited with the winner in the Manchester derby. He's been a firm favourite with United fans ever since. Ryan Wilson, as he was then known (his dad, Danny, was a successful rugby player in the 1970s and 1980s but Giggs reverted to his mother's maiden name when he was 16 as his mother remarried), was first spotted by Dennis Schofield, a milkman and part-time scout who was watching a group of eight year olds play football at Grosvenor Road Primary School in Swinton. "I've been a coach and part-time scout for over half a century," said Schofield, "and he was the best prospect I'd ever seen." Schofield was actually a City fan, but Ferguson was alerted and a few years later he, together with Chief Scout Joe Brown, personally went round to Giggs' house to sign the 14 year old.

"I REMEMBER THE FIRST TIME I SAW HIM. HE WAS 13 AND HE FLOATED ACROSS THE GROUND LIKE A COCKER SPANIEL CHASING A PIECE OF SILVER PAPER IN THE WIND."

PAUL SCHOLES

BIRTH DATE: **16 NOVEMBER 1974**
DEBUT: **21 SEPTEMBER 1994 (VS PORT VALE)**

Paul Scholes signed professional forms in the summer of 1993 but did not break through into the senior ranks until a season later, making his debut in a League Cup match against Port Vale on 21 September 1994. This was the match that produced a plethora of complaints – from Vale, their manager, fans, local press and even an MP – due to Ferguson's decision to field such a youthful side. Hindsight is always 20-20 of course, but in fact the Vale fans present that evening saw a team featuring a number of United players who were destined to become household names. They also, lest it be forgotten, won 2-1. The 19-year-old Scholes – wearing a number 10 shirt that looked like it could comfortably accommodate two of him – scored the first by intercepting in midfield, taking the ball on a couple of strides, then hitting a fierce, swerving shot. He then headed home the winner in the second half. A local boy brought up on the large Langley estate, he played in a Boundary Park Juniors team that included the Neville brothers and Nicky Butt. He didn't play in the 1992 Youth Cup side as there were still a few concerns over his size at that time, though he did play the following year when United lost in the final.

"I THINK PAUL SCHOLES IS THE BEST PLAYER IN ENGLAND. HE'S GOT THE BEST SKILLS, THE BEST BRAIN. NO ONE CAN MATCH HIM. PAUL IS IRREPLACEABLE."

NICKY BUTT

BIRTH DATE: **21 JANUARY 1975**
DEBUT: **21 NOVEMBER 1992 (VS OLDHAM ATHLETIC)**

Nicky Butt was always less high profile than some of his fellow Fledglings, but he became an essential part of the central midfield alongside Roy Keane. Having scored two of the goals in the 3-1 first-leg victory in the Youth Cup Final, Butt made his senior debut on 21 November 1992 when he came on as a substitute in a 3-0 win over Oldham Athletic; the following season he made just two appearances as a substitute; one in the league and one in the FA Cup semi-final, again against Oldham. That game ended in a draw and Butt did not play in either the replay or the final victory over Chelsea. By the beginning of the 1994–95 season, though, he had broken through, and he made 22 starts and 13 further appearances as a sub across all competitions. He also scored his first goal for the club in a 2-2 draw at Southampton. In addition to his 270 appearances for United, Butt played for England at U18, U19, U21 and full levels, playing 39 times for the senior England team. Butt admitted that he hated Gary Neville when he first played against him (for Manchester boys against Bury boys) because Gary never shut up, but once they started training together they just clicked and became great friends.

"NICKY WAS THE FIRST TO BREAK INTO THE SQUAD FROM THAT YOUTH SQUAD. I KNOW WHAT A SERVANT HE HAS BEEN TO ME AND THE CLUB, HE HAS BEEN FANTASTIC."

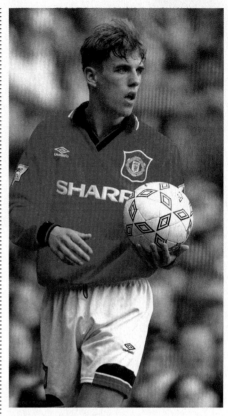

GARY NEVILLE

BIRTH DATE: **18 FEBRUARY 1975**
DEBUT: **16 SEPTEMBER 1992**
(VS TORPEDO MOSCOW)

Gary Neville was a United fan long before he became a player. Many of us thought he would go back to being a fan when he retired. Indeed, he said as much himself: "I'd love just to travel around Europe watching United with my mates. Watching the club you love gives you feelings you can't get from anything else." And no doubt that's where we would have found him had he not become quite possibly the best football analyst on TV – highly thought of even by those supporters who used to hate him as a player. Only four players in history have made more appearances for the club than Gary Neville, who stayed at United for his entire career. Having left school at 16, he signed as an apprentice on £29.50 a week before making his senior debut in September 1992 against Torpedo Moscow in the UEFA Cup (United lost on penalties after two goalless draws). Gary puts much of his success down to his attitude, always being the first to arrive at training and the last one to leave, to compensate for the fact that he wasn't as naturally talented as some of his teammates. Gary captained the 1992 FA Youth Cup team and went on to captain the full side on many occasions throughout his career. He also won 85 caps for the England national team.

"IF HE WAS AN INCH TALLER HE'D BE THE BEST CENTRE-HALF IN BRITAIN. HIS FATHER IS 6FT 2IN – I'D CHECK THE MILKMAN."

DAVID BECKHAM

BIRTH DATE: **2 MAY 1975**
DEBUT: **23 SEPTEMBER 1992**
(VS BRIGHTON & HOVE ALBION)

Unlike the rest of the Class of '92, David Beckham was a Londoner, but both his parents were fanatical United fans who often travelled to Old Trafford for games, and Beckham signed schoolboy forms for the club on his 14th birthday and a Youth Training Scheme two years later. He was deemed too small to play for England Schoolboys but quickly caught up physically and was a major force in the 1992 FA Youth Cup win, scoring in the first leg. This led to a first-team debut early in the following season when he came on for Andrei Kanchelskis in a League Cup match against Brighton. At that stage, Beckham had not even signed professional forms, but he did that on 23 January 1993. In 1994 he played in the aforementioned League Cup game at Port Vale, and in December that year he made a first appearance in the UEFA Champions League, scoring in a 4-0 home win over Galatasaray. He spent a short period on loan at Preston North End before becoming a regular in the 1995–96 double-winning side.

"DAVID BECKHAM IS BRITAIN'S FINEST STRIKER OF A FOOTBALL NOT BECAUSE OF GOD-GIVEN TALENT BUT BECAUSE HE PRACTISES WITH A RELENTLESS APPLICATION THAT THE VAST MAJORITY OF LESS GIFTED PLAYERS WOULDN'T CONTEMPLATE."

PHIL NEVILLE

BIRTH DATE: **21 JANUARY 1977**
DEBUT: **11 FEBRUARY 1995 (VS MANCHESTER CITY)**

Phil Neville is another who wasn't actually part of the 1992 FA Youth Cup-winning side, though like Scholes he did play the following year. Phil was a born leader, captaining his school team at Elton High School, just northwest of Bury, for five consecutive years. But he found it hard to break into the United first team as the full-backs were his brother, Gary, and Denis Irwin. He eventually got his break on 11 February 1995 in the Manchester derby at Maine Road thanks to his older brother's injury. The 18 year old put in a solid performance as United won 3-0 (to add to their 5-0 win at Old Trafford earlier in the season), through goals from Andy Cole, Andrei Kanchelskis and Paul Ince. That was Phil's only appearance in the league that season, but in 1995–96 he played 28 times in all competitions and by the end of that season he had the first of his six Premier League titles. Though versatile and dependable rather than spectacular, Phil played for England at all levels and age groups, including U16, U18, U21 and 'B' team, and went on to win 59 caps for the full England side.

"I DON'T WANT YOU TO LEAVE, THERE'S A CONTRACT THERE AND I WANT YOU TO STAY, BUT I UNDERSTAND FOR YOUR CAREER... YOU SHOULD SIGN FOR EVERTON THAT IS THE BEST CLUB, YOU CAN KEEP YOUR FAMILY UNIT TOGETHER."

THE STORY OF MAN UTD

50
GREATEST
RED DEVILS
OF ALL TIME

Here we salute the best 50 players ever to play for Manchester United. Go on, tell us who we've left out

Words Rob Clark

Any list of Manchester United's greatest players of all time is bound to be subjective. It's impossible to compare across eras for one thing, and we all have a tendency to favour players who stand out in our personal memories for whatever reason. And of course acclaiming individuals in the ultimate team sport is always going to be hostage to the fortunes of the team at the time. How do we weigh achievements against performances during a less successful period for the club? Should longevity and being a one-club man be a major factor? Do we look beyond appearances and goal-scoring records to consider a player's impact at the club, no matter how short-lived? Regardless of how we judge the various parameters, fans always have and always will attempt to compile 'greatest' lists, and it gives us all a chance to recall those staggering moments of skill and perseverance that form our best memories. So here we have a very personal take on Manchester United's best of the best; I know many of you will disagree – and so you should – but it's based on my supporting the club for over 40 years, and writing about them for almost as long.

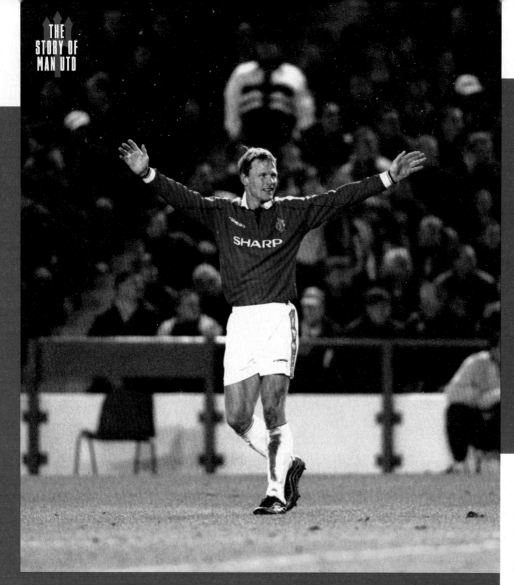

48 STAN PEARSON
1936–1954

Despite losing six years of his career to World War II, Pearson still scored 148 goals in 343 appearances, including a hat-trick in the semi-final and another in the final of the 1948 FA Cup. His movement off the ball brought him many tap ins – and 22 goals in 41 appearances in the 1951–52 league-winning season.

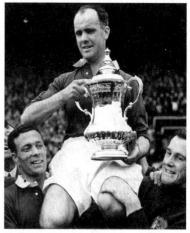

47 JOHNNY CAREY
1936–1953

Irishman Carey was another whose career was interrupted by World War II before returning to claim league and cup titles. Spotted by legendary scout Louis Rocca playing for St James' Gate in Dublin, he was signed for £250 and became an influential figure as club captain.

46 JAAP STAM
1998–2001

 Signed from PSV Eindhoven for a then world-record fee for a defender of £10.75 million, Stam was built like a traditional English stopper but had technical gifts as well. Robbed of his pace by a nasty Achilles injury, United surprisingly decided to cash in on his resale value earlier than might have been expected.

50 TEDDY SHERINGHAM
1997–2001

Sheringham joined in what was assumed to be the autumn of a fine career with Spurs and England only for it to blossom into another summer. Four, to be precise, during which he won three Premier League titles, an FA Cup and a Champions League. He will always be remembered for the equaliser in that final.

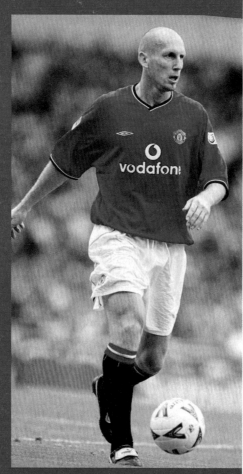

49 HARRY GREGG
1957–1966

Gregg signed from Doncaster Rovers for £23,500 just two months before Munich but stayed at the club for almost a decade more. A brave if unshowy keeper, he suffered numerous injuries but always fought his way back into the side, showing that same resolve that he displayed on a German airfield.

Images Getty Images

45 TONY DUNNE
1960–1973

Signed as a 19 year old from Shelbourne in the difficult post-Munich years, Dunne was another Irishman to have a successful career at United, playing the reliable full-back role in a team packed with attacking talent. He went about his job unassumingly and quietly notched up over 400 appearances.

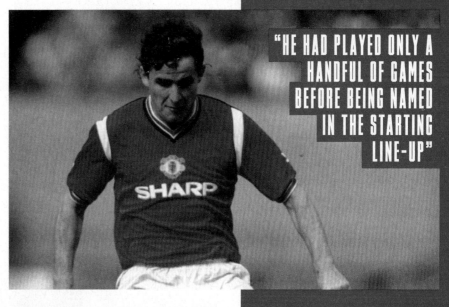

44 BRIAN KIDD
1967–1974

So well known as Ferguson's assistant did Kidd become that it's easy to forget his playing career. Coming through the youth ranks, he started a European Cup final on his 19th birthday. Kidd scored the third goal that day and looked set to take his place in the pantheon of great United strikers, but it never quite happened.

43 DWIGHT YORKE
1998–2002

The yin to Cole's yang, Yorke always seemed to play with a broad grin on his face, as if he were truly loving every minute and couldn't quite believe where he was. His pace, eye for a pass and instinctive finishing were a deadly combination, even if his spell at Old Trafford did prove to be short lived.

42 ANDY COLE
1995–2001

It's as hard to separate Cole and Yorke in the rankings as it was on the pitch, their glorious partnership bringing so many goals – and trophies. There was a suspicion that Cole needed a lot of chances to make one stick, but his goal-scoring record across six seasons speaks for itself.

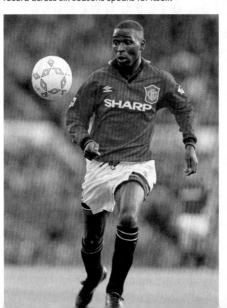

41 ARTHUR ALBISTON
1936–1954

Albiston joined United as an apprentice in 1974, signing professional forms two years later, but he had played only a handful of games before being named in the starting line-up for the 1977 FA Cup Final. He did well against Liverpool winger Steve Heighway and established himself at left-back, making over 480 appearances.

40 PAUL INCE
1989–1995

The self-styled 'Guv'nor' was a combative midfield player who ran hard, tackled ferociously, passed well and could still weigh in with the occasional goal. He misread the room when later signing for Liverpool, which has led to him being less of a fan favourite than he could – and probably should – have been.

THE STORY OF MAN UTD

39 SAMMY MCILROY
1971–1982

Irishman McIlroy was Sir Matt Busby's last signing, making his debut in the 3-3 draw in the 1971 Manchester derby, scoring one and creating the other two. Initially a striker, he reinvented himself as an attacking midfielder, and his longevity at the club owed much to his versatility.

38 LIAM 'BILLY' WHELAN
1953–1958

His death in the Munich air disaster prevented us from seeing just how good Whelan might have become, but at 22 he had already played 95 times for United, scoring 52 goals, and four times for the Republic of Ireland. A skilful winger, Whelan had tricks-a-plenty but end product too as he glided past opponents.

37 MICHAEL CARRICK
2006–2018

A big-money purchase from Spurs, Carrick won an impressive 17 major titles with United, proving a vital cog in the midfield engine room, though he could also step back into defence more than adequately when required. Always calm and seemingly blessed with time, he would frequently control even the highest-pressure games.

36 PADDY CRERAND
1963–1971

A hard-tackling, combative midfielder, Crerand was an important figure in the mid-1960s team when his perceptive passing and endless running kept everything ticking over for the superstars up front. Later assistant manager to Tommy Docherty and then a regular at club TV station MUTV, Crerand is United through and through.

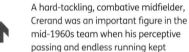
"HE MADE HIS DEBUT FROM THE BENCH IN A 4-0 WIN"

35 STEVE COPPELL
1975–1983

Part of the long-standing tradition of exciting wingplay at Old Trafford, Coppell was a highly regarded right wing whose speed and work rate were a major asset in the years of only moderate success. A Liverpudlian, Coppell initially played for lower league side Tranmere Rovers so he could continue his education via an economics degree. But the wages United offered him were too good to turn down, and he made his debut from the bench in a 4-0 win over Cardiff City on 1 March 1975 – United were in Second Division that season. A horrific knee injury suffered while playing for England against Hungary all but finished his career at just 28.

34 PAUL MCGRATH
1982–1989

McGrath rose from a difficult background, which included time in foster care and an orphanage, to become a truly great defender. He had power, pace and touch and was equally assured in the air and on the ground. The fact he looked in control all the time on the pitch provided a stark contrast with his time off it, where he needed alcohol to ward off his shyness and dislike of the limelight. A combination of alcoholism and knee surgeries led to Ferguson selling him to Aston Villa, where he later reunited with Ron Atkinson and had a successful 'second' career, culminating in him winning the 1993 PFA Players' Player of the Year Award.

33 BRIAN McCLAIR
1987-1998

'Choccy' McClair joined United in July 1987 for £850,000 after four successful seasons at Celtic, where his goal-per-game ratio was considerably better than one in two – often quoted as the measure of a world-class striker. McClair quickly proved he wasn't just a flat-track bully and was equally capable of scoring hatfuls in the English First Division, becoming the first player to net more than 20 goals in a season for United since George Best 20 years earlier. That his goal-scoring feats became fewer owed much to him being moved around, eventually back into midfield, but his versatility made him indispensable to his manager.

32 OLE GUNNAR SOLSKJÆR
1996-2007

The Norwegian made his name at home club Molde before a £1.5-million transfer during the Euro 1996 tournament. Solskjær quickly made a name for himself and was soon nicknamed 'the baby-faced assassin' by fans for his combination of youthful good looks and deadly striking. Tactically astute, he was able to analyse games from the bench and made a habit of coming on late in games and scoring, most notably his four in ten minutes against Nottingham Forest in February 1999 and of course the Champions League winner that same season. His 'Olegend' status has not been diminished by his underwhelming stint as United manager.

31 EDWIN VAN DER SAR
2005-2011

United had targeted Van der Sar as a replacement for Peter Schmeichel in 1999, but instead he went to Juventus and then to Fulham, so it was another six years before he came to the club. When he did, he established himself as one of the very best keepers, saving a penalty during the 2008 Champions League Final, which led to him becoming one of a select number to win Europe's premier club competition with two different clubs. Slim but tall and athletic, he had excellent positional sense and could distribute the ball accurately with either foot. He won 26 major honours across the teams he played for and gained 130 caps for the Netherlands.

30 GARY PALLISTER
1989-1998

Pallister grew up a Middlesbrough supporter in County Durham and signed for the club when he was 19, going on to make over 150 appearances. He moved to United in August 1989 for £2.3 million, a record fee for a defender at the time. He proved worth it, making over 300 appearances for United at the heart of the defence. Having not previously played in the top flight, Pallister was initially prone to the odd lapse of concentration, but once he had ironed that out he became a powerhouse. A back injury suffered at the end of the 1995-96 season robbed him of a little pace. He returned to Middlesbrough to see out his career.

29 NORMAN WHITESIDE
1982-1989

Born in Belfast and growing up in poverty on Shankill Road, Whiteside was a footballing prodigy. Legendary scout Bob Bishop persuaded Whiteside to sign, though initially the youngster remained in Belfast, flying to Manchester for training at weekends. He made his first-team debut as a 16 year old and scored his first goal, in a 2-0 win over Stoke City, a mere eight days after he turned 17. He's the youngest goalscorer in both an FA Cup and League Cup final. Whiteside was strong, fearless, good with both feet and in the air and blessed with a cool temperament; the only thing he lacked was a yard of pace due to his constant knee and pelvic injuries.

28 PATRICE EVRA
2006-2014

Born in Senegal, Evra only lived there for the first year of his life before his family moved to Belgium and then France. Evra was a street footballer who started out as a striker before being moved to the wing and eventually full-back, though he never lost his instincts to get forward or to make overlapping runs on the wide left. Originally, several clubs rejected him for being too small, but he was physically strong and tactically smart. After bouncing around various French clubs he found his true home at United, signing in January 2006 and going on to make over 270 appearances and win 14 major trophies.

27 STEVE BRUCE
1987–1996

Bruce was a hugely popular figure at United, as much for his whole-hearted approach and his captaincy credentials as his playing style, which could occasionally be described as 'agricultural'. A late starter who had all but abandoned hope of playing professionally, Bruce was well into his twenties before attracting attention from the top clubs. He signed for United at the end of 1987, just before he turned 27, and his determination brought him over 300 appearances and a handful of very important goals. Famously never capped by England, a strange omission, Bruce has since had a solid managerial career.

26 MARTIN BUCHAN
1972–1983

Buchan was exactly the sort of player United needed as they sought, successfully, to bounce back after relegation, his strength of character and leadership being just as important as his play. Captain for six years, Buchan was the first man to captain both Scottish and English Cup-winning sides – he led Aberdeen to victory over Jock Stein's Celtic in 1970 – and was a star of the 1977 victory over Liverpool, in which he calmly marked Kevin Keegan out of the game. Buchan made over 450 appearances for United, along with 34 for Scotland, despite playing in the years when both club and country were not at their most successful.

25 MARK HUGHES
1980–1986 & 1988–1995

Welshman Hughes' time at United was more eventful than most, encompassing two separate periods. Born in Wrexham, 'Sparky' joined United straight from school, having been spotted by the club's North Wales talent scout Hugh Roberts. He didn't make his first team debut for three years but then scored 37 goals in 89 games before being transferred to Barcelona. He returned to United two years later and went on to make a further 256 appearances and score 83 goals. A quiet soul off the pitch, on it Hughes was a rampaging force of nature. The fans loved his whole-hearted endeavour and spectacular volleyed goals.

24 NEMANJA VIDIĆ
2006–2014

Looking to all the world like a shaven-headed Eastern European gangster, Vidić bulked up and quickly adapted to Premier League life after joining in January 2006. Often described as 'no nonsense', Vidić was the perfect foil to the elegant Rio Ferdinand, the brick-wall stopper who wasn't interested in bringing the ball out of defence, just preventing anyone from running through it. His positional sense and combativeness were much prized by Ferguson and team-mates alike, as was his bravery in putting his head in when he knew he was likely to get clattered. Vidić played over 200 matches for United, won 15 major trophies with them and was named in the PFA Team of the Year on four separate occasions.

23 DENNIS VIOLLET
1953-1962

Viollet came through the ranks at United and turned professional in 1950, when he was 17, although he didn't make his first-team debut for a further three years. Lightning fast, he was the perfect foil for Tommy Taylor's more physical presence, and together they terrorised defences and scored hatfuls of goals – Viollet's 32 in a 36-game First Division in 1959–60 remains a club record. He was surprisingly sold to Stoke in 1962, having scored 179 goals in 293 appearances. Manchester born, but a City fan, Viollet moved to America to coach and was instrumental in establishing their professional league.

19 BILL FOULKES
1950–1970

Foulkes was the archetypal stopper; a big, rugged man who played at the centre of defence and for who the phrase 'none shall pass' might have been coined. Fourth on the all-time appearances record with 688, he was discovered at 18 playing for Whiston Boys' Club. Born in St Helens, both his father and grandfather had played rugby league for their hometown club. Not convinced he was good enough to play football professionally, Foulkes continued to work part-time as a miner, only stopping after winning his first (and ironically only) England cap. Powerful in the air and solid on the ground, Foulkes was a fitness fanatic who worked hard on his game but remained resolutely low profile throughout his 20-year career.

18 DENIS IRWIN
1990–2002

Vying with Roger Byrne for the title of United's best left-back, Irwin might have been an understated player, but his team certainly appreciated the value he brought to the side. Winner of seven league titles, together with three FA Cups, a League Cup, a Champions League and a Cup Winners' Cup, Irwin boasts an impressive haul of trophies. He made a huge impact playing for Oldham Athletic, helping the team reach the final of the League Cup and semi-finals of the FA Cup in 1990. United somehow acquired him for only £625,000, an absolute steal for a man who would go on to make 368 appearances.

21 NOBBY STILES
1960–1971

Stiles was a defensive midfielder who did the 'grunt' work of winning and retaining possession, enabling the ball-players such as Best and Charlton to thrive further forward. A teenaged England Schoolboys international at the time of Munich, Stiles was devastated by the loss of his heroes and determined to live up to their memories. Although unprepossessing in appearance – Stiles was short, ungainly, very short-sighted and prematurely balding – he was an invaluable rock in the sort of holding midfielder role that was virtually unknown in the 1960s. He played almost 400 games for United and is one of only three Englishmen to have won the World Cup and European Cup.

17 TOMMY TAYLOR
1953–1958

How good might Taylor have become? It's impossible to say for certain, but in his 191 games for United he scored 131 goals, and for England he scored 16 goals in 19 games. As Taylor was only 26 when he died at Munich, he could easily have played another four or five years at the highest level, and if he had maintained a similar strike rate he would have been the club's all-time leading scorer. A big, physically imposing man, Taylor had a bullet header and a physical approach that – like many of the best strikers – intimidated defenders. A Barnsley boy, Taylor was wanted by many of the big clubs, but Matt Busby got him in March 1953 for the sum of £29,999.

22 DAVID DE GEA
2011–

The tall Spaniard was initially deemed too lightweight for the physical challenges presented by the English Premier League and looked too easy to intimidate, but he has worked hard on becoming a more dominant figure on crosses. Always there was his supreme shot-stopping and athletic ability to get to the ball, even in the corners of the goal. During a largely unsettled period for the club, he has saved them so many times that his record transfer price of £18.9 million has been made to look a bargain. Four times he has been voted the club's player of the year, and five times he has featured in the PFA Team of the Year.

20 RUUD VAN NISTELROOY
2001–2006

One of the most prolific strikers to play for United, Dutchman van Nistelrooy's goal-scoring exploits earned him 11th place in the club's all-time top scorers list. And that was in just five seasons – a decade at the club with a similar games-to-goals ratio would have seen him comfortably top that chart. Van Nistelrooy started life as a central midfield but was moved up front by his first professional club, Den Bosch. He then spent a year at Heerenveen before three at PSV Eindhoven, where he scored a ridiculous 62 goals in 67 matches. Fast, strong and with an opportunist's eye for the goal, he was a lethal finisher.

16 ROGER BYRNE
1951–1958

Byrne was naturally right-sided, but his work rate and footballing intelligence in terms of positioning was such that he could play in a number of different positions, including wing-half and outside left. But it was as a left-back that he made his name with United – and England. United scout Joe Armstrong saw something in him, and he was offered first amateur, and soon after, professional terms. He had charisma and leadership potential, and the Busby Babes would follow their team captain wherever he asked them to go. In the ensuing seven seasons he played 245 times for the club. He also played 33 consecutive matches for his country, appearing in every England fixture from his first call-up against Scotland in April 1954 to the 4-0 win over France in November 1957.

15 GARY NEVILLE
1992–2011

Neville was United through and through, from his days as a youngster on the terraces to his one-club professional career with 400 appearances. A tenacious right-back, Neville was recognised for his hard work and his professionalism, with his lack of natural flair occasionally leading observers to overlook his consistency and solid dependability. He ploughed the furrow up and down the right flank for years, often giving his friend Beckham room to manoeuvre. He did the same for England, winning 85 caps and being described by Ferguson as the "best English right-back of his generation". A commanding presence on and off the pitch, Neville was a born leader and the sort of player fans of opposing teams love to hate. It's a measure of his tactical ability that a decade after his retirement he is now recognised as one of the most astute analysts of the game in media.

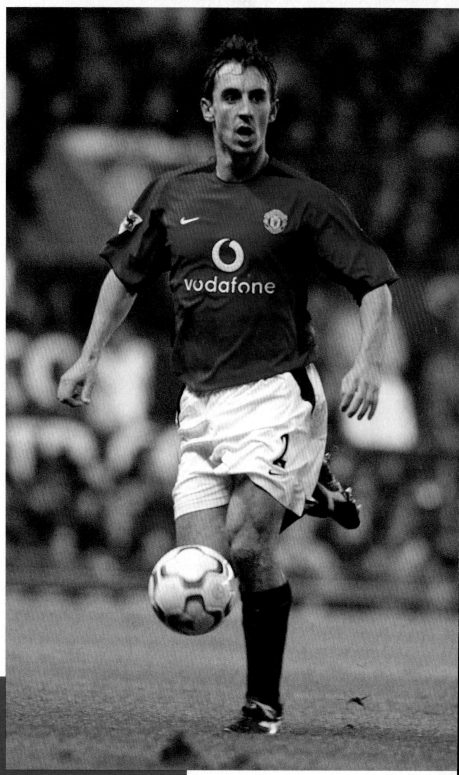

14 DAVID BECKHAM
1993–2003

Fittingly, Becks sits right in front of Neville, as he did so many times for United and England. In more recent times it seems to have become acceptable to be overly critical of Beckham – whether for his fashion sense, celebrity wife or good looks. But make no mistake, Beckham was a very serious footballer, a relentless trainer who supplemented his god-given skill at striking a dead ball – from corners and free kicks – with a range of passing and crossing that had few equals. His career took off after he scored from his own half against Wimbledon in August 1996. He earned 115 England caps.

13 ROY KEANE
1993–2005

Every top club needs a Keane, a midfield enforcer who won't shy away from confrontations and breaks up opposition attacks by fair means or foul. Keane certainly wasn't averse to fouls, and his fierce temper was never far from erupting, but he was an essential player for United. Born in a suburb of Cork, Keane started his career at semi-professional club Cobh Ramblers before being spotted by Nottingham Forest, who he represented for three seasons. Upon Forest's relegation, Keane activated a break clause in his contract; he was all set to sign for Blackburn Rovers until a last-minute swoop by Ferguson saw him go to Old Trafford for a record £3.75 million. Keane could never stay away from controversy for long, but his blood and thunder approach remained popular.

"RONALDO CAN DRIBBLE AND PERFORM A HUGE ARRAY OF TRICKS AT SPEED"

12 CRISTIANO RONALDO

2003–2009 & 2021–2022

 The best player to have played for United, the sole reason he doesn't feature higher up is that most of his best years were played elsewhere. One of the fastest men in football, Ronaldo can dribble and perform a huge array of tricks at speed, in particular a bewildering number of step overs. He's also strong in the air, boasting a hang time that appears to defy gravity. CR7 has always been a showman, leading to accusations of arrogance, but he's won the league and cup in England, Spain and Italy. Records include most appearances (183) and most goals (140) in the Champions League, most goals in the European Championship (14) and most international goals (118) and international appearances for a major nation (196).

11 RIO FERDINAND
2002–2014

 We perhaps underrated Rio when he was at the club; everyone acknowledged his speed and skill, his positional sense was superb, his timing immaculate and his discipline impeccable, but still there was a sense that he was just doing what good defenders do, mopping up at the back and giving the defence an air of solidity, possibly because he seemed more European in style than English, being comfortable in possession and calm about playing out from the back, either through distribution or his own running. But he very rarely made a mistake in his prime years, and when he did he had the speed to make a recovery tackle. Ferdinand went to the West Ham youth academy then into the first team there before moving to Leeds United in November 2000. Two seasons later he joined United for a fee of £30 million. He's now recognised as one of the all-time great defenders for club (over 300 appearances) and country (81 caps).

50 GREATEST RED DEVILS

10 PAUL SCHOLES
1991–2013

Another who played his whole career at United, and what a career it was! Scholes has won everything in the game, including an almost-inconceivable ten Premier League titles. Scholes first started training with United at 14, although he wasn't part of the 1992 FA Youth Cup-winning side as there were still concerns about his small stature. His technical and ball-striking ability soon came to the fore, though, and his range of passing, clever movement on and off the ball and vision for the game made him the complete midfielder. Fellow midfield greats sung his praises, while Thierry Henry once described him as the greatest player in Premier League history. Scholes played over 700 times for United, scoring 155 goals. He had no interest in a celebrity lifestyle and has always lived out of the limelight away from football, but on the pitch he's one of the all-time stars.

09 WAYNE ROONEY
2004–2017

There's sometimes a sense that Rooney was a supreme talent not wholly fulfilled, but in truth those reservations really belong to England. In the red of United he was a phenomenon, blasting onto the stage as an 18 year old to score a hat-trick in a Champions League match with Fenerbahçe and going on to win every major club honour. Rooney was born in Croxteth in Liverpool and grew up as an Everton fan. He was associated with the club from the age of nine, but Everton's precarious financial position forced them into a sale, and in August 2004 he moved to United. On his signing, Denis Law declared that Rooney would "have all the United records", and in terms of goalscoring, at least, he was proven right. His 253 goals make him United's leading goalscorer, and he is behind only Alan Shearer as the Premier League's top goalscorer. He also has 103 assists, placing him third in the all-time list. Quite possibly the last 'street' footballer.

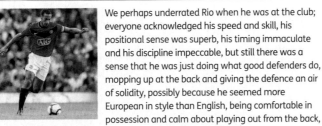

Images Getty Images

08 PETER SCHMEICHEL
1991–1999

How many clubs would have a goalkeeper in their top ten players of all time? The answer to that is probably 'any club for which Peter Schmeichel played'. The great Dane enjoyed success at Brøndby before being picked up by United in August 1991 for £505,000, a price described at the end of his time at the club as the "bargain of the century" by Ferguson. Schmeichel was tall but not exceptional for a modern goalie, but his ability to spread himself and 'make himself big' in the face of an onrushing forward often created a barrier that was impossible to breach. In particular, Schmeichel would perform 'star jump' saves where his arms and legs would all be spread as wide as possible to fill any gaps. Schmeichel was also mentally strong and could come up with important saves in a game where he had spent the majority of the time as a spectator. His distribution was also excellent, and he could turn defence into attack with one throw.

> "HIS ABILITY TO SPREAD HIMSELF AND 'MAKE HIMSELF BIG' IN THE FACE OF AN ONRUSHING FORWARD OFTEN CREATED A BARRIER THAT WAS IMPOSSIBLE TO BREACH"

07 DUNCAN EDWARDS
1953–1958

It's hard to assess just how good Edwards was, as he was only 21 when he died at Munich, and unfortunately very little footage of him remains. But we should listen to what his contemporaries said of him, including Busby, who described him as "the most complete player in Britain, and possibly the world," and Charlton, who said he was "the best player I have ever seen. The best player I played with, for United or England." Edwards was equally adept with either foot, strong, powerful in the air and physically dynamic, with a range of passing few have ever equalled. At the time of his tragic death, Edwards had already played 177 times for United, scoring 21 goals, having joined as a teenager and making his first-team debut at 17. He'd already played 18 games for England. At his funeral it was said that "talent, even genius, we will see again. But there will only ever be one Duncan Edwards."

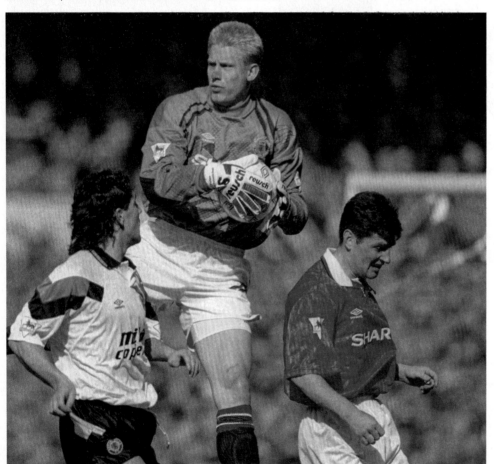

06 DENIS LAW
1962–1973

Law was born in Aberdeen and grew up in poverty in a council house where shoes were considered a luxury. His talent for football was a way out, and he seized the opportunity with both hands, first with Huddersfield Town and Manchester City, then with Torino in Italy and back to Manchester, this time with United, for who he debuted on 18 August 1962. Law's time at the club largely coincided with a fallow, post-Munich period, so his honours of two league titles and an FA Cup – though he was famously injured

> "HE IS THE JOINT TOP ALL-TIME SCORER FOR SCOTLAND"

for the European Cup final – vastly understate both his importance and his ability. But as a goal-scorer, Law was 'The King', notching 237 of them in 404 games, including 34 in 46 FA Cup games and 28 in 33 in Europe. With 30 goals in 55 games, he is the joint top all-time scorer for Scotland, matching Kenny Dalglish, who took 102 caps to notch the same total.

05 ERIC CANTONA

1992–1997

"CANTONA WAS AN INVETERATE TRAINER, DEDICATED TO HIS CRAFT"

→ More than a few good players have wilted when they came to United. The club, and its history, are just too big for some people. Cantona was the opposite. He swaggered in, stuck his chest out, raised his head and surveyed everything as though he were asking, 'I'm Cantona. Are you big enough for me?' If ever there was a player that was made for United, it was Cantona. The story of how he came to Old Trafford is legendary; it started with a casual enquiry from Leeds United about the availability of Denis Irwin and ended with the maverick forward signing for United for £1.2 million. In fairness to Leeds, most commentators felt it was good business – Cantona was talented but wayward, and none of his previous clubs had kept him happy for long. People looked at him, shirt collar turned up, insouciance personified, and saw a dilettante. It was nonsense. Cantona was an inveterate trainer, dedicated to his craft and frequently found doing extra sessions. That attitude rubbed off on the young players around him, who grew up thinking it was the norm. In his five seasons at the club they won four league titles and two FA Cups, gaining the self-belief that would lead to many more, for which Cantona was the catalyst.

04 BRYAN ROBSON

1981–1994

"HIS LIST OF PERSONAL HONOURS ISN'T AS BIG AS IT SHOULD HAVE BEEN, BUT HIS COMMITMENT TO THE CAUSE CAN NEVER BE DOUBTED"

← Younger United fans might find it hard to believe we ever had a box-to-box midfielder better than Roy Keane. But those of us who were around when Robson was in his prime know that we did. Robson was Captain Marvel, a man with a ridiculous engine, capable of breaking up play in his own box and still being on the end of a cross into the opponent's box seconds later. His peak came before Ferguson's great league-winning sides, so his list of personal honours isn't as big as it should have been, but his commitment to the cause can never be doubted. The only problem with Robson was that the team were overly reliant on him, and his regular bouts of injury meant that he did miss games – sometimes important ones. Robbo played 461 times for United – scoring 99 goals, a decent return for a midfielder – but could have played so many more. He was United's longest-serving captain and always led by example. Robson also played 90 games for England, in 65 of which he was the captain, scoring 26 goals. Manager Bobby Robson described him as "as good a player as we've ever produced".

THE STORY OF MAN UTD

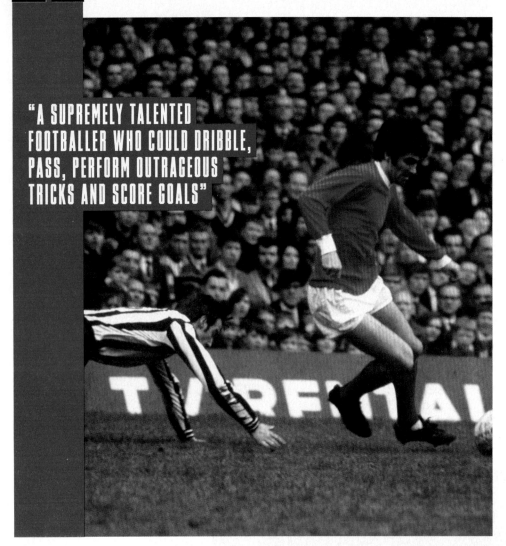

"A SUPREMELY TALENTED FOOTBALLER WHO COULD DRIBBLE, PASS, PERFORM OUTRAGEOUS TRICKS AND SCORE GOALS"

03 GEORGE BEST

1963–1974

Best was the man who originated the Number 7 legend at United, making the shirt an icon of skill, desire and status. Among its wearers have been Ronaldo, Cantona, Beckham and Robson. But Best was the best of the lot, a supremely talented footballer who could dribble, pass, perform outrageous tricks and score goals. Busby once said of him that he was the best at everything at the club – best tackler, fastest runner, hardest shooter, most skilful... And as with Cantona years later, the flamboyance was backed by a work ethic that meant Best was a great trainer. He scored 179 goals in 470 matches – an impressive number for a player who was not an out-and-out striker and was rarely the beneficiary of a tap in. Many of them are memorable, owing to his sublime touch and insane ball control, which enabled him to dribble past defenders and round goalkeepers. Best had his problems off the pitch, wanting to outdo everyone there as well as on it before finally succumbing to his destructive streak, but as José Mourinho famously said, "Players like George Best never die. What they leave behind them never dies." Anyone who saw Best at his peak will attest to the truth of that verdict.

02 BOBBY CHARLTON

1953–1973

Charlton was more than a great player; he was the rock on which the club was anchored in the dark days after Munich, the one constant (even above Busby) who kept the club afloat, kept the dream alive and dragged the club back to the pinnacle of the sport. For a long time Charlton was at the head of both the all-time appearances list (758) and the all-time scorers list (249), and though he's now slipped into second place on both, behind Giggs and Rooney respectively, it's still a mark of the player as to how long and successful his United career was. Born in Northumberland, Charlton signed to the club as a 15 year old on 9 February 1953, although his mother insisted he start an apprenticeship as an electrical engineer in case the football didn't work out. Strong and well balanced, with a piledriver of a right foot – though he was genuinely two-footed – Charlton was equally at home in midfield or up front. He always carried with him the pain of losing his friends and team-mates, but he paid them homage in the best way possible by winning the European Cup.

"IT'S STILL A MARK OF THE PLAYER AS TO HOW LONG AND SUCCESSFUL HIS UNITED CAREER WAS"

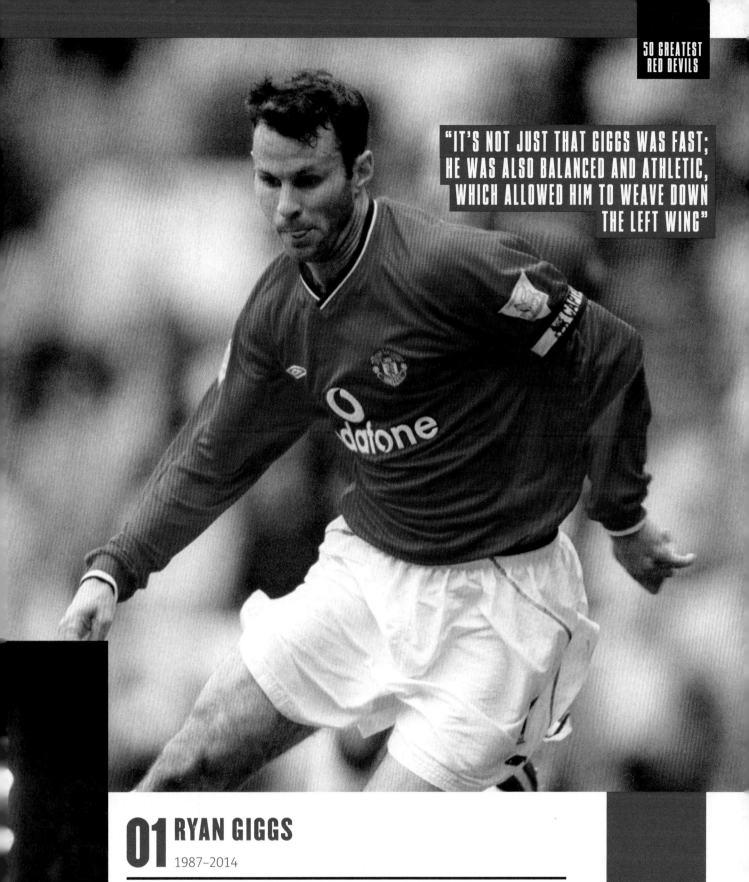

"IT'S NOT JUST THAT GIGGS WAS FAST;
HE WAS ALSO BALANCED AND ATHLETIC,
WHICH ALLOWED HIM TO WEAVE DOWN
THE LEFT WING"

01 RYAN GIGGS
1987–2014

The Welsh winger made more appearances in a United shirt than anyone else (963) and stands equal seventh on the goalscoring list (168) despite playing as a winger, or latterly a midfielder. Unsurprisingly given his crossing ability, he also holds the record for the most assists in the Premier League. Born in Cardiff but brought up in Salford, Giggs is very much a Manchester boy and the epitome of a one-club man. He won 13 league titles, two Champions Leagues, four FA Cups, four League Cups, the Club World Cup, the Intercontinental Cup and the UEFA Super Cup; he is the most decorated British footballer in history. But set aside his longevity and his honours and consider his football. It's not just that Giggs was fast; he was also balanced and athletic, which allowed him to weave down the left wing beating players for pace or for skill, to go wide or to cut back in. Frequently dubbed 'the new George Best' when he exploded onto the scene as a 17 year old, Giggs, unlike Best, also had the mental fortitude and temperament to cope with both the acclaim and the criticism. His acceleration and ability to change direction while running at top speed led Ferguson to declare that he left defenders with "twisted blood". A footballing phenomenon.

OOH, AHH, CANTONA

They didn't make them like Eric then, and they still don't now. Unapologetically enigmatic, the Frenchman spent his career thrilling and befuddling in equal measure – no one in football history carries an aura like the King. Cantona wowed, warred and often wounded, but thank God he came here 30 years ago

Words Chris Flanagan
Additional reporting Nicolas Puiravau, Ian Murtagh

Midway through the 1991–92 season, Michel Platini strode up to the boss of one of England's biggest clubs and began his sales pitch.

"I've got a player for you," he told the man stood in front of him, a fearsome Scot who'd enjoyed managerial success north of the border but had yet to steer his current team to a league title in England. Platini believed he knew just the person who could seriously improve their fortunes.

"He's a problem boy, but he's also really talented," said the French legend, then the coach of the national team. "He'd be perfect for your club."

Graeme Souness wasn't so sure. Liverpool were ninth in the top flight, their glory days fading to grey. That night, they'd beaten Auxerre at Anfield in the UEFA Cup, but that hadn't softened Souey's mood. The answer was an immediate no.

"Listen Michel," he said, "I'm fighting fires at the moment, trying to get some people out the door. They're resisting – I'm fighting

a dressing room. The last thing that I need is another controversial figure in there."

Liverpool had just turned down the chance to sign Eric Cantona. A few weeks later, in December 1991, the France international announced his retirement at the age of 25. Banned for a month for throwing the ball at a referee, the Nimes forward responded to the disciplinary panel by approaching each member and uttering the word 'idiot' in their direction, one by one. When the suspension was then doubled, Cantona called it quits.

Thankfully, his retirement didn't last long. On 8 February 1992, a day after the expiry of his two-month ban, he was making his debut for Leeds United at Boundary Park against Oldham Athletic. Nine months later, he joined Manchester United... and the rest is history.

While Liverpool would go three decades without a league title, Cantona helped their biggest rivals end their own 26-year top-flight drought in 1993 and begin a glittering era of incredible dominance. Thirty years after his arrival on these shores, this is the inside story of the man who changed English football.

1966 WAS A GREAT YEAR...

Born in May 1966, he was raised in Marseille by father Albert – a painter of Italian heritage – and mother Eleonore, whose parents had left Spain during the Civil War. Cantona was a 14 year old turning out for his junior side Caillolais when he met his footballing mentor.

"Eric already had that way of standing very straight, that haughty stance," long-serving former Auxerre boss Guy Roux remembers as he talks to *FourFourTwo*. "He looked like a prince at a ceremony alongside the Queen of England.

"He came to my attention via someone I'd sent to a trials event in Aix-en-Provence. They told me about a phenomenon, tall and physically strong, who already had all the qualities needed. We immediately tried to get him to Auxerre. He'd already had a lot of trials, particularly at Nice, but agreed to come to our club with a dozen other kids.

"At the end of the ten-day training camp, we put him into a short eight-vs-eight match with our first-team professionals and he was excellent – even if some of them criticised him for dribbling too much. We could already tell that there was a fire inside him.

"I met him face to face and asked him if we could get him something he'd like. He told me about a jersey, so I sent him to the club shop where he was given a jersey, some shorts and socks. I later learned that he'd made the same request at Nice, and they'd charged him for it."

Cantona signed for Auxerre, initially staying in a lodge that once housed local monks near the city's cathedral. He didn't exactly live like a monk, though, even then.

"He was the most difficult [to manage]," Roux admits. "He had a late childhood and a turbulent adolescence. His training was under the guidance of Daniel Rolland, and we managed Eric between us.

"I remember an argument he had one afternoon with one of his best friends,

Stephane Mazzolini. The two started chasing each other and they ended up in the dining hall, with Cantona trying to catch him. They jumped from table to table, overturning all the plates, cutlery and glasses. A massacre!

"Eric was the band leader – not of a mafia gang but of a cheerful little group who were mostly successful on the field. Later on, one match in Lens was postponed because of fog, so we travelled directly to Saint-Brieuc to prepare for a game at Brest. In the evening, we went to the town hall at Roscoff, a small town in Brittany twinned with Auxerre. At the end of a small ceremony with the mayor, I realised that seven players had disappeared. We sat down to dinner and I was facing a window, through which I saw them coming back. They were all around Cantona, who'd shaved his head – he had no more hair.

"Cantona was staying in a room opposite mine, and that night I heard him talking to his girlfriend, complaining that his head was cold. For their little night out, I sanctioned

them two weeks without going out. But the next day, we played Brest and won."

Cantona's first-team debut came at 17, in 1983. He'd already appeared for France's under-17s, although the Foreign Office had to step in to defuse a diplomatic incident after he'd travelled to Leningrad for a youth tournament and spat at the referee – an officer in the Soviet army. As was mandatory for French teenagers back then, he also had to carry out national service, delaying his progress with Auxerre.

"He was in the Joinville battalion," Roux explains, referring to a special military unit for sportsmen. "One day, the colonel of the battalion called and told me that a general was coming for an inspection. He said that Cantona didn't shave well, and asked me what to do. The only solution we found was to send Eric to get potatoes and get him home late, so he didn't run into the general!"

Cantona returned for more brief first-team appearances in 1985, scoring his first senior

"ERIC DIDN'T SHAVE WELL. WE SENT HIM TO GET POTATOES SO HE WOULDN'T RUN INTO THE GENERAL"

Papin tells *FFT*. "It was already Eric Cantona – we knew what he could bring to a team, and we quickly gave him the reins."

Briefly drafted back to the U21s for a vital European Championship semi-final against England, he darted from the halfway line, past Martin Keown & Co in the Three Lions defence, to score in a 4-2 win in Besancon. At Highbury in the second leg, he netted twice more – defeating Paul Gascoigne in the duel of the emerging mavericks, as Les Bleuets went on to become continental champions.

At club level, though, Cantona became embroiled in not one but two controversial incidents – the first with Auxerre's own goalkeeper. "One morning, there was eight centimetres of snow on the pitch, so I sent the players to clear it using the advertising boards," Roux says. "Cantona was pushing like crazy, but Bruno Martini was resting a little. The tone rose, then Eric ended the discussion with a nudge." Or, to put it less diplomatically, a headbutt.

In April 1988 in Nantes, an astonishingly high two-footed tackle on defender Michel Der Zakarian earned Cantona a red card and two-month suspension. "Those two got into a dispute – I later learned they were from the same neighbourhood in Marseille," Roux says. "For Eric, it was OK to tease each other once in a while, but we're talking about a tackle at hip height! Sometimes it was hard to hold him back. After that tackle, he returned to the changing room and the stadium caretaker fled – he didn't want to bump into Eric…"

COVERED IN KETCHUP

Despite the controversies, Marseille shelled out a French record fee of around £2m to sign the 22 year old that summer. Everyone knew the talent the volcanic maverick possessed.

"All the big French clubs were interested, including Monaco, Paris Saint-Germain and Matra Racing," says Roux. The latter are now known as Racing Club and play in France's fifth tier but had just finished seventh in the top flight back then and were spending big to progress further. "Matra Racing invited him for dinner, and Eric asked me how he should dress. I told him not to put on his jeans with the four stab wounds at the knee, but a suit. He didn't have one so went to buy one. Matra Racing had a row of French-style guards to welcome him – he was excited.

"Then one evening, I got a call from Bernard Tapie at Marseille, asking if he

---

goal against Rouen in mid-May before fizzing in a 25-yard thunderbolt against Strasbourg a fortnight later that confirmed Auxerre's qualification for the UEFA Cup. To gain more experience he was then loaned to Martigues, a few miles outside of Marseille.

"I'd learned that every Saturday night, he got into his car after Auxerre matches and went to see his girlfriend in Martigues – it was a 600km journey, and I was afraid it would end in a dramatic accident," Roux explains. "During 1985–86, Martigues were last in the second division, five points behind their rivals, but I thought a loan would be good for Eric, and he did too. He helped them stay up."

Cantona was also sent off twice – first for a tiff with one fan who'd insulted him, then receiving his marching orders again when Martigues were already safe from relegation.

"Martigues played Cannes – a friend of Eric's played for Istres, and if Martigues won then it helped Istres to stay up," Roux says. "He'd promised his friend that Martigues

Above Guy Roux was Cantona's first footballing mentor, working hard to rescue his protégé from a few sticky spots

would win, but quickly he realised that his team-mates weren't playing very hard and got angry with them. One of the Cannes players told him to calm down, and Eric shot him an upper cut. He got a three-match suspension, which he had to serve at Auxerre because his loan was over. But I went to see the president of the federation, told him what had happened, and the suspension was overturned by a presidential amnesty."

Back at Auxerre, Cantona struck 17 goals in 1986–87. "He'd become an adult," says Roux, who managed the club for an incredible 41 years. "We often talk about Maradona's goal against England at the 1986 World Cup, but Eric did similar things with us. He'd start from midfield, dribble around everyone and score. He was already an exceptional player."

In August 1987, Cantona made his debut for France at senior level, scoring in a friendly against West Germany after starting upfront alongside Jean-Pierre Papin. "We lost 2-1 in Berlin, but Eric scored just after half-time," could come and see my phenomenon. We arrived at Cantona's house at around 8 p.m., and Eric was painting. Tapie asked Cantona where he was born, and Cantona said Marseille. Tapie said, 'Well, that's it – you're coming to play in Marseille, then'."

L'OM got their man after outbidding their rivals and fending off late competition from Milan. "We needed players like Cantona," says Papin, who'd joined Marseille two years earlier. But Cantona remained sceptical of Tapie. "There were things about Marseille he didn't like," Roux says.

His time at the club started badly, too – left out of the France squad after a goalless first month, he responded by branding national team boss Henri Michel a "s**tbag", insisting he wouldn't play for Les Bleus again while Michel was in charge.

By January, Cantona was starting to forge a partnership with Papin, but his relationship with Tapie had deteriorated – then he threw his shirt away and marched off topless after being substituted during a charity match against Torpedo Moscow, arranged to raise funds after an earthquake in Armenia. Marseille banned him for a month and Tapie suggested Cantona needed psychiatric help, so the player boarded a plane to Barcelona, his grandfather's home city. He was loaned to Bordeaux for the rest of the campaign.

At the start of 1989–90, Cantona was again loaned out, to Montpellier, but then recalled to the France squad by new boss Platini, who was eager to harness his talent and salvage an ailing World Cup qualifying campaign. On Eric's return, both he and Papin bagged braces in a 4-2 win in Sweden.

"Platini knew football well, and he knew Eric and I could play together – we'd already done it at Marseille," Papin says. "I scored a lot of goals thanks to Eric, and he did too. We just complemented each other. It was never easy for the opposition to control him – he often had one or two defenders permanently on him, which allowed me to find space and use my speed."

Cantona bagged eight goals in eight games for France that season, even if Les Bleus still missed out on Italia 90. With ambitious Montpellier, he'd score 14 times and win the Coupe de France, despite a difficult start to the season when they were dragged into a relegation battle.

"There was talent in that team, but the atmosphere wasn't ideal," says their former midfielder Jean-Claude Lemoult. "A lot of responsibilities were given to young players, and that was complicated. Whether it's in a changing room, a movie or just in life, Eric is very prominent. He has ideas, views and he's not shy about expressing them. Reporters often came to talk to him, so he could say what he had to say."

With old foe Michel Der Zakarian now also a team-mate, perhaps another flashpoint was always inevitable.

"We lost 1-0 at Lille, and when we returned to the changing room I was talking to Michel," Lemoult says. "Cantona came over and got angry – I tried to calm him down by telling him that we weren't talking about him, but he threw a boot in my face and a fight broke out. The president wanted to fire him, but he met Eric a few days later, they had a chat and in the end he didn't."

Instead, it was manager Aimé Jacquet – later a 1998 World Cup winner with France – who was soon fired and replaced by Michel Mezy. Lemoult and Cantona put their scuffle behind them, and Montpellier went on to lift their first major trophy for 61 years.

"Eric had an important role in us winning the Coupe de France, particularly in the semis

"I TRIED TO CALM ERIC DOWN, BUT THEN HE THREW A BOOT IN MY FACE AND A FIGHT BROKE OUT. THE CLUB WANTED TO FIRE HIM"

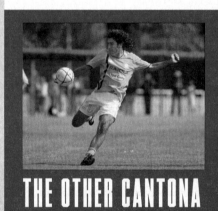

THE OTHER CANTONA

A year after Eric's arrival in England, his younger brother turned up too.

Joel Cantona began his career with fleeting appearances for Marseille, leaving in 1987 – a year before Eric arrived. Joel joined Rennes, Antwerp, Angers and then Hungarian side Ujpest, before heading to Peterborough United in 1993.

That didn't work out, so he joined third-tier Stockport, playing a handful of games and displaying some typical Cantona eccentricity – ahead of the 1994 Second Division Play-off Final, he treated those travelling by coach to a random but nevertheless memorable rendition of *All That She Wants* by Ace of Base, in a thick French accent.

Having returned to Marseille, relegated after their infamous match-fixing scandal, he retired early like big bro, leaving *l'OM* at 28.

Clockwise from left Eric took after his painter father; a lethal Papin pairing; flying to the Coupe de France **Clockwise from right** "Hats, not hate"; on loan at Montpellier; "I think *bleu* is my colour"

against Saint-Etienne," Lemoult says. "That fight between us was just the consequence of disappointment after a defeat, nothing more – we were separated and it ended there. I later became team-mates with him again at Nimes; it was Eric who advised the club to take me."

Cantona returned to Marseille for 1990–91, initially scoring regularly alongside Papin. "He was never the slightest problem in the dressing room," his strike partner insists.

Papin even got away with accidentally squirting an entire bottle of ketchup over him during a mealtime prank, of which Chris Waddle had been the intended recipient. Team-mates held their breath, expecting Cantona to explode, but instead he carried on eating as if nothing at all had happened. "Everyone who was there still remembers it!" Papin smiles.

Injury halted Cantona's progress, though – by the time he returned, Raymond Goethals had replaced Franz Beckenbauer, and boss and forward didn't see eye to eye.

Marseille won the league and reached the European Cup final, but Cantona didn't even make the bench having been frozen out from March onwards. *L'OM* were defeated by Red Star Belgrade on penalties after 120 goalless minutes of 'action'.

"It's a regret that he didn't play the final with us," Papin says. "I tried to use my role as captain to talk to the coach, but Goethals was a bit stubborn. The reason for Eric being sidelined wasn't sporting, even if the coach told us otherwise.

"But Goethals made it clear to me that he'd made his choices, and he didn't have to discuss them. We'll never know if we would have won that final with Eric in the team, but he never disappointed in big games. I think it could have been a very big day for him."

Cantona never played for Marseille again – he was sold to Nimes for around £1m and installed as their new captain. The French firebrand was reunited with old Montpellier boss Michel Mezy, but joining a promoted club was risky for a 25 year old who was still France's first-choice forward.

Nimes started the season poorly, and Cantona quickly grew frustrated. Platini sounded out Liverpool, attempting to find a better home for his key man, before the forward went nuclear. During a home game against Saint-Etienne in early December, Cantona grabbed the ball and hurled it at the referee after an innocuous free kick had been awarded against him.

"He left the field even before he was sent off," says Lemoult, his team-mate once more at Nimes. "I didn't see the incident coming, but Eric was unpredictable. Everyone knew it wasn't difficult to annoy him on the pitch – a lot of opponents did. He hated injustice and couldn't control himself."

A one-month suspension was dished out at his disciplinary hearing, then increased to two months after Cantona insulted the panel. As he later said, "They passed judgement on my life as a whole, not just the isolated incident, so I told them they were idiots, which was remarkably restrained for me."

"We didn't see him at the club for a while," Lemoult says. "He locked himself in his house, tormented by that episode. I went there to eat with him, and I also tried to make him understand that he had to keep going. But he wanted to end his career."

ERIC CANTONA'S INDOOR LEAGUE

A few days before Christmas 1991, Cantona announced his retirement from football. Only Platini's intervention changed his mind, after the French boss insisted that a transfer to England could be the solution. There, he was virtually unknown and could start afresh, without the past weighing him down.

So, in late January, Cantona travelled to Yorkshire for a stint training with Sheffield Wednesday on an artificial pitch because of freezing weather conditions. His only public appearance for the Owls came at the new Sheffield Arena, in a scheduled six-a-side Transatlantic Challenge clash against visiting US team Baltimore Blast of the Major Indoor Soccer League.

Part of a Wednesday line-up that also contained Graham Hyde, Chris Bart-Williams and American international John Harkes, grainy YouTube footage tells us that Cantona scrabbled around on a tiny pitch, attempting to force the ball into a miniature goal from two yards. Perhaps unsurprisingly, Baltimore and the Major Indoor Soccer League both folded later that year.

Like Nimes, Wednesday had just been promoted to the top tier. Unlike Nimes, they doubted they had the budget to actually sign Cantona. "A former agent of mine asked if I'd do a favour to Platini, who was very keen to

Above "Ou est 'Oldham'?" **Below** Cantona won the Charity Shield and First Division while a Leeds player

get Cantona back playing," Owls boss Trevor Francis later revealed to the *Yorkshire Post*. "He wondered if I'd have a look at him in training. I said, 'I don't really need another centre-forward, but as a favour, I'll do it'.

"I was surprised when he arrived – it was built up as if I was looking to sign him, which was never a consideration. He was here to do a few days' training, basically putting himself in the shop window. There was this indoor tournament – so I asked him if he wanted to play, and he had a kickaround.

"After those two days it was put to me, 'Are you going to sign him?' I said, 'Well, I don't think so, we'd like him to stay for a few more days for us to have a little look at him'.

"I think his manager took that as an insult – I don't know if it was a breakdown in communication, but they regarded it as he was Eric Cantona and he was not going to be on trial. The whole thing got messy, and he came to me and said, 'I've got a chance to go to Leeds'. He had my blessing."

Spearheaded by 18 goals from David Hirst, Wednesday went on to finish third, but then Cantona ended up as a champion at Elland Road, joining on loan from Nimes until the middle of April for £100,000, with the option to make the deal permanent for £1m.

"To begin with, I don't think any of us really knew who he was – these were the days before the internet," admits Jon Newsome, a member of that title-winning squad. "He was quietly spoken and didn't speak much

"ERIC PICKED UP THE MICROPHONE AND SAID 'I DON'T KNOW WHY, BUT I LOVE YOU' TO 250,000 LEEDS FANS. THAT WAS HIM"

English, but he joined in with things and his quality was there for everybody to see. Physically, you could see that he'd be able to handle the demands of the Premier League – anything that was thrown at him in training, he could deal with."

Leeds were already top when they travelled to Oldham in early February 1992, but they'd fallen behind at Boundary Park by the time Cantona was brought on for his debut and lost 2-0. With Lee Chapman and Rod Wallace already established as a strong partnership up front, the Frenchman only started one of his first six games – coming on as a sub to score against Luton. But when Manchester United moved two points behind Leeds with three games in hand after the Whites fell 4-1 at QPR in March, manager Howard Wilkinson trialled a new system that incorporated all three of his forwards.

The trio all scored in a 5-1 home win over Wimbledon, when Cantona wore the No.3 shirt, but the next three games delivered only two points; Manchester United took control at the top and Leeds' new signing returned to the bench. He responded with a sensational cameo at home to Chelsea, assisting Chapman before scoring a breathtaking effort of his own – juggling the ball one way and then the other before firing home.

"He turned the centre-half inside-out and then stuck it in the top corner," Newsome remembers. "He was incredible on his day."

Wilkinson swiftly confirmed Cantona's permanent signing – the Chelsea triumph kick-started Leeds' form as they overtook Manchester United again and won the title. Cantona had scored just three times, but he'd had some influence in the club's only league championship since 1974.

"A while back, I saw a Sheffield Wednesday fan say on Twitter that if they'd kept hold of Cantona, they'd have won the league because he went to Leeds, scored loads of goals and won us the title," Newsome says. "That was harsh on the lads who played 35 or 40 games that season, because Eric scored three goals and started six games. But he was the cherry on the icing on top of the cake, a little sprinkling of stardust, and on occasions he did something that changed the game.

"He was a good lad to be around. When we won the title, they built a stage for us on the steps of the city hall, and we stood there with the trophy – they reckon there were 250,000 there. Eric picked the microphone up and said, 'I love you – I don't know why, but I love you'. We all looked at each other as if to say, 'Where's that come from?' but that was him. He knew what to say and how to say it."

THE FORMULA 1 CAR ARRIVES

Cantona lined up for France at Euro 92 – the only major tournament of his career – but couldn't find the net as Les Bleus went out in the group stage, drawing 0-0 with Graham Taylor's England in their second match.

Back at Leeds, he scored nine times in his first seven appearances of the new campaign – netting a hat-trick in the Charity Shield

against Liverpool, before repeating the feat in a home game against Spurs to become the first player to bag a Premier League treble. In the new Champions League, he scored in a September knockout tie against Stuttgart, later replayed at the Camp Nou after Leeds' German rivals were found to have fielded an ineligible player.

Within a couple of months, however, Eric was gone. While struggling to repeat their title-winning form, Leeds lost to Rangers at Ibrox in the second round of the Champions League – the Frenchman couldn't make an impact and walked straight down the tunnel after being substituted. He was dropped for the next match at QPR.

"Rangers was the start of his downfall," Newsome remembers. "History has shown that Eric was a very headstrong individual, and under Howard Wilkinson you all had your own roles to play on the field. If you didn't do what he asked you to do, it was quite simple: he'd get someone else to do it and you wouldn't be playing. It was things like the defensive side of the game, and not putting the ball at risk. But Eric wanted to do things his own way.

"Howard and Alex Ferguson are two very different people, and they handled him in two very different ways. By the time we played QPR, it was obvious Eric and Howard weren't seeing eye to eye. He went off early in training with an injury, and rather than seeing the physio, he went home. Then there was one pre-match meeting at the hotel he turned up late to and didn't have the correct attire. They were all statements by Eric to either annoy the manager or force his way out."

Cantona returned to Leeds' line-up for the second leg against Rangers and even scored, but the Whites went out anyway. Then they lost 4-0 at Manchester City in early November, slipping to 14th in the Premier League, before exiting the League Cup at second-tier outfit Watford. Cantona was dropped again and handed in a transfer request, demanding to join Manchester United, Liverpool or Arsenal.

Wilkinson tried to find a buyer in Italy, Spain or France, but he found no takers. Then came the most pivotal phone call in Premier League history, from Leeds' managing director Bill Fotherby to Manchester United chairman Martin Edwards, enquiring about signing Denis Irwin. By chance, Alex Ferguson was sat opposite Edwards and passed him a note that read, "Ask about Cantona."

Manchester United were only eighth in the league, nine points behind leaders Norwich, having hit just 17 goals in 16 games – fewer than three of the bottom four. Ferguson had missed out on Alan Shearer to Blackburn in the summer, then signed Dion Dublin from Cambridge, only for the targetman to break his leg in cruel fashion.

The Scot responded by trying to sign Hirst from Sheffield Wednesday, for what would have been a record fee paid by a British club. "I can still hear Alex now on my car phone, totally exasperated because he'd put in two offers that I'd knocked back," Trevor Francis said. "I refused £4m and Alex bellowed down the phone, 'Do you realise this is

"MY DAD HAD DENIS LAW, BUT CANTONA WAS OURS"

Stephen Howson, from the *Stretford Paddock* YouTube channel, explains what Eric means to his generation

....

Timing is everything, and no timing has ever been better than Eric Cantona's arrival at Manchester United.
The chemical reaction that occurred when he met Sir Alex Ferguson, when his arrogant confidence spread to the fledglings of the youth team, hasn't been replicated since. Emerging from the darkness of the 1980s, United needed a spark to become a '90s behemoth. Cantona was it. Talent-wise, there have been better Premier League players. As a captain, he was no Roy Keane. But Cantona brought a certain joy to the game, mixed with his raw aggression, undeniably world-class ability, and of course, that arrogance.

He was signed at my ninth birthday party. Literally. My party was at the club museum on the day of Eric's unveiling, which forced my festivities to be cut short. They gave me his shirt to make up for it – the shirt he held on the pitch that day.

It was my third season watching football, and I was beginning to properly understand the game. I'd had a couple of favourite players by then – Paul Ince mainly, don't judge – but I was ready to properly fall in love with the sport... and with this club. I grew up watching Eric Cantona. I carried his confidence into school. Every collar I wore turned up.

I was 11 when he kicked Matthew Simmons and delivered the seagulls press conference. What did it mean? Not a clue. Did I repeat it to my mum when she asked why I was in trouble at school? Yes. Did it work? Obviously not.

To Reds of a certain vintage, Cantona is God. I even took his flag to Afghanistan when I served in the armed forces. My dad had the Lawman, and the European Cup of 1968. Our uncles had the Doc's Red Army. Cantona was ours.

I met him in 2017, and I've never been as nervous in my life. To explain him using stats and tactics would be like explaining love to a tin of beans. He transcends the sport. He's a cultural figure. He told you himself, he's not a man. He's Cantona.

Manchester United Football Club, you're stopping a player going to Man United?'"

Cantona was a different type of player, arrived at almost by accident, but Leeds let him leave for just £1.2m. Or so Whites fans thought, anyway: Edwards later revealed on BBC documentary *Fever Pitch* that the fee was in fact £1m but publicly declared higher to avoid Fotherby getting too much stick.

"When he joined us, the club was a bit like a Formula 1 car – it just needed a Formula 1 driver to steer it, and Eric was that man," Gary Pallister tells *FFT*. "He was the final piece of the jigsaw, a perfect fit. The day he walked into the United changing room is still fresh in my memory.

"We were all a bit sceptical because of his reputation, wondering what kind of individual was joining us, but the moment he arrived, he had that aura – and it transmitted onto the pitch straight away.

"No one I can think of ever hit the ground running like Eric did. He had this real unique quality and understanding of the game, and gave us the imagination we'd perhaps lacked. From day one, he was outstanding."

"HE WANTED TO KILL THAT F**KER"

After making his first Manchester United appearance against Benfica in Lisbon, in a December friendly to mark Eusebio's 50th birthday, Cantona soon partnered Mark

"WE WERE ALL A BIT SCEPTICAL BECAUSE OF HIS REPUTATION, BUT HE JUST HAD THIS AURA"

Hughes up front in the Premier League, with Brian McClair moved into midfield.

The Frenchman quickly scored four in four games – equalising in a draw at Chelsea, then bagging the leveller as they came from 3-0 down at Sheffield Wednesday. One goal and two assists in a 5-0 thrashing of Coventry soon followed, before a header as United hammered Tottenham 4-1. That was the day Cantona also delivered a sumptuous assist for Irwin, extravagantly flicking the ball over Spurs' defence with the outside of a boot, in

Clockwise from above Cantona ended 26 years of hurt; a rare fashion *faux pas*; "Eric who?"; getting into hot water in Turkey

a way that only Cantona could. He later claimed it was his favourite moment of his whole United career. In little more than a month, Eric had catapulted Ferguson's side to the top of the table.

"The way he played was different from anyone else – he was a genius," Pallister says. "But it wasn't just on the pitch that he settled in seamlessly. He really loved being among the lads.

"He was a different character – he'd talk about poetry and paintings, and also refer to a game as a blank canvas for him to perform a work of art. He was a bit different from the typical raggy-arsed footballer from a working class background! But the beauty of Eric was that he embraced all of our foibles, too.

"It's well known that the United lads had a bit of a drinking club going. We called them team meetings, and they often lasted until kicking-out time. A lot of foreign lads came to

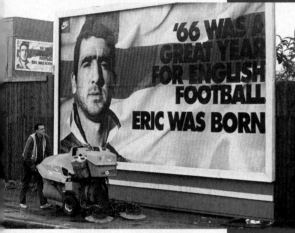

without incident – he spat at some home fans during the 0-0 draw and was fined £1,000 by the FA. Chasing their first league title for 26 years, the Red Devils dropped back to third, behind Norwich and Aston Villa, after a run of four matches without a win. In April, a trip to Carrow Road had the whiff of a title decider.

Cantona helped Ferguson's side destroy the Canaries on the counter-attack – playing in Ryan Giggs for the opener, then scoring himself to make it 3-0 after just 21 minutes. It began a run of seven straight victories that sealed the Premier League – Cantona had won the league for a third successive season with a third different club, and this time he'd been absolutely crucial.

The 1993–94 campaign would bring with it another Premier League title and 25 goals in all competitions – his highest ever tally. Arguably Cantona's best league strike was a missile of a free-kick at home to Arsenal as United surged clear at the top very early on.

Outside of England, things went less well. The Frenchman had scored in a 3-3 home draw with Galatasaray in the Champions League, then United travelled to Istanbul for the second leg, greeted by 'Welcome to Hell' banners at the airport. In an incredibly hostile atmosphere at the Ali Sami Yen, they drew 0-0 to exit the competition in November 1993, and Cantona was sent off after the final whistle for lambasting the referee. He was escorted off the pitch by a policeman, who then punched him in the tunnel.

"Eric went crazy in the dressing room," Roy Keane later said. "The rest of us just wanted to get out of there, but he was determined to go back outside to sort out the rogue cop. He insisted he was going to kill 'that f**ker'. It took the combined efforts of Brian Kidd and a few players to restrain him. Normally I wouldn't have backed off a fight, but even I wasn't up for that one. There were a lot of Turks out there."

A fortnight later, Cantona put France ahead in their final qualifier for the 1994 World Cup – his sixth goal of the group – only for Bulgaria to hit back and win 2-1 in Paris,

eliminating Les Bleus. "Eric is one of the greatest players in French history – we scored a lot together during that qualifying campaign," Jean-Pierre Papin says. "Our partnership should have reached its full potential at the World Cup in the United States. Unfortunately, we missed out on getting there."

Cantona took third place in the Ballon d'Or, beaten only by Roberto Baggio and Dennis Bergkamp, then started to propel United to the FA Cup final – he bagged a stunning volley against Wimbledon at Selhurst Park, minutes after Vinnie Jones had almost cut him in half with an outrageous tackle. If he reacted with surprising calmness then, the same wasn't true in the Premier League at Swindon – Cantona was sent off for stamping on John Moncur after a tussle, before getting dismissed again at Arsenal three days later, this time for a second bookable offence.

United lost two of the three games he missed through suspension, as Blackburn drew level at the top – Ferguson's men had been 16 points clear of them at one stage. But Cantona returned with both goals in victory over Manchester City, and guided his side to their first ever double by scoring two penalties in the FA Cup final against Chelsea.

Before the first, Chelsea skipper Dennis Wise had wagered £50 that he'd miss. "£100," Cantona responded, before slotting the ball into the corner with trademark ease, having waited for Dmitri Kharine to dive. He offered Wise double or quits before the second one, then scored in identical fashion.

"He was a maverick, but he trained like a beast every day – and by God, he did the business, especially in the big games," Bruce tells *FFT*. "Cup finals, semi-finals... when you needed a goal, Eric came up trumps. The bigger the game, the more he enjoyed it."

FERGIE ON A HARLEY-DAVIDSON

Cantona became the first overseas star to win the PFA Player of the Year Award in 1993–94, although his summer was as eventful as ever.

England and disapproved of that culture, but Eric absolutely loved it because he wanted to feel part of the squad. He gave as good as he got during those sessions – at the end of the night, he'd often be the one asking when we planned our next meeting..."

Cantona's lifestyle was relatively modest, as well. "Once, I remember one of the papers did an article on the houses we were all living in," Steve Bruce tells *FFT*. "I'm sure quite a few people were surprised to find that Eric lived in a little terraced house in Worsley and drove a Honda Prelude – nothing flash. I remember him coming into training and asking, 'What's all this about? Why the fuss?' We said, 'Maybe they think you need a bigger house'. He said, 'Why? I have a house in Barcelona, I also have a house in Marseille – so I don't need a big house here'."

Cantona's return to Elland Road with Manchester United in March 1993 wasn't

LIFE'S A BEACH

After leaving Manchester United, Cantona dipped his toes into a host of activities...

ACTING
Cantona first threw himself into a different kind of drama career during his ban for the Selhurst Park kung-fu kick: playing a rugby player in French film *Le Bonheur Est Dans Le Pré*. He later became a regular on Nike adverts, hosting the star-studded cage tournament before the 2002 World Cup, as well as pretending to

be a farmer for Kronenbourg. Cantona even appeared in Oscar-nominated movie *Elizabeth* and in a Liam Gallagher music video (left), but his most famous role was as himself in *Looking For Eric*, the 2009 Ken Loach film that he also co-produced.

BEACH FOOTBALL
Cantona became the captain of France's beach football team and had taken over as manager by the time they won the

inaugural World Cup in Rio in 2005. After 14 years with the team, he resigned in 2011 following relegation from the top division of the Euro Beach Soccer League.

NEW YORK COSMOS
In the same year that he departed beach football Cantona headed for the US to become the director of football at a relaunched Cosmos, citing an ambition to help them become one of the world's best clubs. He was later sacked after punching a photographer then won damages for unfair dismissal.

Not long after being appointed France captain by new boss Jacquet, he was arrested in the US, where he was scheduled to do media work, for an altercation about accreditation before Brazil's World Cup semi-final against Sweden. Then another miserable trip to Ibrox followed; sent off in a pre-season friendly, Eric would begin 1994–95 suspended.

Cantona was also banned for United's first four games in the Champions League group stage, following that Galatasaray dismissal. Thrashed 4-0 at Barcelona without him, the Red Devils lost at Gothenburg on his return and missed out on the knockout phase. In the Premier League, however, he struck 12 times in 21 games – an even better strike rate than the previous campaign.

Midway through January, in his first match alongside new signing Andy Cole, he bagged the winner against title rivals Blackburn, which hauled United to within two points of the top. But then came the fateful game at Crystal Palace, the red card for kicking Richard Shaw, and a kung-fu assault on the fan who hurled vitriol at him as he walked off.

"Sometimes when the red mist comes down, we all make mistakes, and he paid a high price for that one," Bruce admits. "I'm sure Eric regrets it – or maybe not! If you asked him if he'd do it again, he'd probably say yes."

True to form, the man himself once told *FFT* about his only regret from that incident. "I didn't hit him strong enough. I should have punched him harder," Cantona said. "If I want to kick a fan, I do it." Punch, hit, kick – same difference, eh?

He was sentenced to two weeks in prison but an appeal reduced his punishment to 120 hours of community service, which was spent coaching kids at United's training ground. That appeal verdict produced possibly football's most famous 14-second press conference. "When the seagulls follow the trawler, it is because they think sardines will be thrown into the sea. Thank you," he memorably declared, before getting up and strolling out the room.

Cantona's words baffled the world, his United team-mates included. "Our reaction was the same as everyone else – we hadn't a clue what he was on about!" Bruce laughs.

THE PALACE FAN: WHAT HAPPENED NEXT

It wasn't just Eric who had his collar felt after the kung-fu kick. So did the recipient...

The court drama surrounding Eric Cantona's kung-fu kick stretched beyond the Frenchman – Matthew Simmons got in on the act, too.

The Palace fan was hauled to Croydon Magistrates Court and then fined £500 for his role in the Selhurst Park incident, found guilty of threatening behaviour.

After hearing arguments that he should also be handed a one-year stadium ban, he didn't respond well – jumping over the bench and then grabbing the prosecutor by their neck. "This is a lie, I'm innocent I promise, I swear on the Bible," Simmons shouted.

As police and court staff tried to restrain him, he then battled his way over to watching journalists, calling them 'scum'. Then only 21, he was sentenced to seven days in prison for contempt of court.

Simmons, who'd previously been on National Front rallies, went on to join the Territorial Army.

"The papers were asking, 'Is he mad? Is he crazy?' We did ask him what it was all about, and to this day, I still remember his reply. He said, 'I don't know where it came from, but it was f**king good, wasn't it?'"

Aimed at the media flock who'd followed his every move since that Selhurst flare-up, the Frenchman had written his line on a piece of paper beforehand after asking the club's baffled head of security what the correct English words were for a fishing boat and the small fish in the sea.

"Hundreds of journalists were there, and the club's lawyer wanted me to say something," Cantona recently explained, launching his new travel brand, Looking FC. "I didn't want to say anything, but he said, 'You have to'. I just said what came to mind. I could have said 'the sky is blue' or 'I saw a lion flying'. But I said that and left.

"I think the journalists were happy, and I was very happy because they all tried to understand what I'd said. They'd treated me like I was a criminal – I never killed anybody. Thousands of times, I'd heard fans say things and never reacted. This time I reacted – I'm not a robot, and I never wanted to be a robot. Sometimes I'm good, sometimes I'm bad. Sometimes I'm sweet, sometimes I'm s**t."

There was never any chance of his United team-mates ribbing him for his ostentatious quotes, though.

Above From panto villain to kung-fu assassin – the ten seconds that created his United legend

"No one took the mick out of him, ever," Bruce says. "Not because we were scared of him, but because he had the respect of the dressing room. He'd earned that with his performances on the pitch."

Cantona had also earned the affection of his manager, who'd already settled on a sensitive man-management style for the team's biggest star. Ferguson had previously enjoyed several conversations with Guy Roux about him, even visiting Cantona's mentor at Auxerre to glean information.

On the night of the kung-fu kick, the United boss directed his post-match hairdryers to Cantona's team-mates for letting a 1-0 lead slip, rather than balling out the Frenchman.

"The boss came into the dressing room and was fuming," Lee Sharpe said. "We look at each other, thinking, 'F**king hell, Cantona is getting it here!' He says, 'Incey, where the f**k have you been? Sharpey, my grandmother runs f**king faster than you! You're all a f**king disgrace. Nine o'clock tomorrow morning, I'm going to run your f**king balls off in training. F**king shocking. And Eric... you can't go round doing things like that, son'."

United moved quickly to suspend Cantona for the rest of the season, hoping it would be enough to prevent further punishment from the FA. It wasn't: Cantona was banned for

eight months. Jacquet also stripped him of the national team captaincy – after 20 goals from 45 caps, he never played for France again, his lengthy absence allowing Zinedine Zidane to emerge as Les Bleus' new star. Without Cantona, United were pipped to the title by Blackburn in 1994–95, before their star man vowed to quit English football when the FA announced that they were investigating a behind-closed-doors friendly match against Rochdale, believing it may have contravened his ban. United insisted it was only a training game, but Cantona went AWOL, feeling the FA were being unfair.

Inter were interested in taking him to Serie A, but he agreed to return to Manchester after the FA relented and Ferguson dashed to Paris to track him down, riding around the streets on the back of a Harley-Davidson with Cantona's lawyer.

On 1 October 1995, Cantona made his much-anticipated return, setting up Nicky Butt, then converting a penalty in a 2-2 draw with Liverpool. "It was a long eight months for Eric – it was written in the stars that he'd score when he came back," Bruce smiles.

FAREWELL, FEATURING RICHARD KEYS

With Paul Ince, Mark Hughes and Andrei Kanchelskis all sold that summer, a young United side had famously lost the opening game of the season at Aston Villa, prompting Alan Hansen's famous declaration, "You can't win anything with kids." The Reds had also gone out of the UEFA Cup to Rotor Volgograd.

Manchester United trailed Newcastle by 12 points at one stage, but Cantona's return had provided leadership for the emerging Class of '92, before he struck the winner at St James' Park in early March 1996. Cantona scored in six consecutive matches – levelling in Fergie Time at QPR, then netting winners against Arsenal, Spurs and Coventry, plus a goal and two assists in a 3-2 triumph at Manchester City. In those six games alone, his individual contribution had earned United 12 points – enough to overhaul the Magpies at the top.

Once more, he helped United to the double, firing in from the edge of the box in the FA Cup final against Liverpool to clinch a 1-0 win then lifting the trophy as captain in place of the injured Bruce. Before the presentation, though, he'd tried to persuade the centre-back to do the honours.

"A lot of words have been written to try to describe Eric over the years, and I'll give you two more – kind and considerate," says Bruce. "For me, that gesture at the cup final summed him up, and showed what a man he was. He'd just scored a late winner, but he approached me and said, 'Come on, you've got to lift the cup'. I said, 'Listen Eric, if anyone deserves to do that, then it's you. I've done it before – it's your turn now. Thanks for the offer, but this is your moment'."

Savaged by the press 16 months earlier, Cantona was named as the Football Writers' Association's Footballer of the Year and then appointed as captain on a permanent basis when Bruce departed for Birmingham.

On a visit to England, Roux saw how much Cantona was adored. "He was the King of Manchester," the 83 year old smiles. "I met him to make a documentary – when he stepped on to the pavement, there were 200 people around him. It was amazing to see."

United were playing catch-up again in 1996–97 – nine points behind Liverpool just before Christmas, when Cantona scored a sublime hang-it-in-the-Louvre goal in a 5-0 home win over Sunderland. After dribbling from the halfway line, he exchanged passes with McClair before brilliantly chipping keeper Lionel Perez, then stood arms outstretched, accepting the adulation as if to ask, 'Are you not entertained?' Maximus Decimus Meridius and *Gladiator* were still four years away, but Leeds fan Russell Crowe was taking notes.

"I can't think of another player who played with Cantona's swagger," says Pallister. "The way he played with his collar up, and that celebration against Sunderland. Imagine anyone else doing that – we'd never have got away with it. We'd have had the piss ripped out of us! But he carried it off superbly."

Cantona later said that the celebration was aimed at Perez, a former Nimes team-mate, who'd feared people might disapprove if he was too friendly with the United star before kick-off. "Before the game, I went over to say hello," Cantona said. "He didn't want to shake my hand, so maybe that's why I scored that goal. That's the biggest humiliation for

"WE COULDN'T HAVE WON THOSE TROPHIES WITHOUT HIM. WE'D ALL LIKE TO BE ERIC CANTONA"

a goalkeeper, and that kind of celebration, too. I just stand there. Look at me."

United fought back to win the league once more – Cantona's sixth title in seven seasons. It might have been seven in seven were it not for the kung-fu kick. But a day after they were beaten by Borussia Dortmund in the 1996-97 Champions League semi-finals, the King told Ferguson he would be retiring at the end of the season, aged only 30.

"I admire a player that can play at the same club for 20 years like Ryan Giggs, Paolo Maldini or Xavi," he later said. "I'm not that type of person. I get bored very quickly. I was very passionate about the game, and always said that when I lost that passion, I would retire. It just went like a light switch."

Cantona's retirement plan stayed a secret until the campaign was over. After providing an assist for Jordi Cruyff in a home win over West Ham, on the day United lifted another Premier League trophy, his last fixture as a professional came in a post-season benefit match for David Busst – Cantona scored twice against Coventry at Highfield Road on a night

Clockwise from top Celebrating *that* beautiful Sunderland chip; "Who hurtled around Paris on a Harley?"; Eric broke Geordie hearts in 1996

that also featured cameos from Gazza and, er, Richard Keys.

Then came the announcement of his exit. "Retiring at 30? Ridiculous!" says Bruce. "But that's Eric – he did things his way. Could we have won the trophies that we did without him? No, absolutely not. He was the catalyst, exactly what we needed. He was a great, great player. A born winner. In a way, we'd all like to be Eric Cantona."

Cantona packed more into his career than most other players combined. Before him, United hadn't won the league in 26 years. With him, they won it four times in five seasons, laying the foundation for nine more triumphs to knock Liverpool off their perch.

Eric Cantona was the man who started it all. Arguably, he's the most significant player in almost 30 years of Premier League history. Turns out Graeme Souness should probably have signed him after all.

MORE ON FOURFOURTWO.COM

- Why Eric Cantona meant so much to Manchester United fans *(by Andy Mitten)*

- Eric Cantona answers your questions: "I didn't hit the Palace fan strong enough. I should have punched him harder" *(by Andy Mitten)*

- Year Zero: The making of Eric Cantona, 1992-93 *(by Nick Moore)*

MANCHESTER UNITED

Words Sam Pilger

DOMINATE THE '90S

After ending their 26-year wait for the title in 1993, United enjoyed the start of their most successful era

After Manchester United had come so close to winning their first league title for a quarter of a century the previous season, an acute sense of disappointment lingered with Ferguson and his players throughout the summer of 1992.

"It was a really terrible time; a horrible feeling stayed with me for months," former United captain Steve Bruce has recalled. "We knew we were the best team in England and it was now up to us to prove it, but that disappointment was really hard to shift in the opening months."

While Ferguson had attempted to inspire his squad with bold words about how they would find strength in their despondency and how their failure would make them better men, there was little evidence of that when the 1992–93 season kicked off. At the dawn of the new Premier League, United took just one point from their opening three league games, which included worrying defeats to both Sheffield United and Everton.

Ferguson's side would rally with five consecutive league wins in August and September but slump in the autumn and go on a run of seven league games without a win to leave them tenth in the table.

The major problem was United's lack of goals, which had severely undermined their title challenge towards the end of the previous season and was once again hurting them.

Ferguson had unsuccessfully attempted to sign Alan Shearer from Southampton in a bid to bolster his forward line, the Geordie striker instead moving to Blackburn Rovers, and he also failed to tempt David Hirst from Sheffield Wednesday.

Instead, Ferguson had to be content with bringing in a less-heralded striker in Dion Dublin from Cambridge, but he would break his leg in September to add to United's glaring weakness.

At the start of November 1992, following three league games without scoring, Ferguson knew he had to act, and after getting nowhere with Hirst again, the United manager was surprised to learn that Leeds United were willing to sell their enigmatic French striker, Eric Cantona.

United quickly signed Cantona for just £1 million, and as Ferguson has reflected, "One of the most extraordinary periods in the history of Manchester United was about to begin."

"Eric had an impact on all of us; he lifted us, gave us belief and led us towards the title," said Bruce. "He was a great trainer, professional and athlete, and he brought an aura that demanded the best."

Cantona would himself score nine league goals and also bring out the best in his new team-mates. Before he arrived, United had scored 18 goals in 17 games, but with him they would net 49 goals in 25 games, earning him the nickname of 'the can-opener' from Ferguson.

Within a month United went top of the Premier League, and, after fending off the challenge of Aston Villa, they were there at the end of the season to become league champions for the first time since 1967.

"It was the day I truly became manager of Manchester United," Ferguson has said. "It was the historic moment when I could finally realise, even inwardly accept for the first time, that I was the man in charge. There was a sudden, overwhelming realisation that now I was master of my own destiny."

A newly emboldened Ferguson used this to guide United to their first-ever league and FA Cup double the following season, with a side many still contend was the greatest in the club's history.

It featured a starting 11 that fans can recite with ease: arguably the game's greatest-ever goalkeeper Peter Schmeichel, protected

Below Ryan Giggs in thrilling full flight playing against Ipswich Town in May 1994
Bottom Roy Keane lifts the Premier League trophy aloft, 8 May 1994

by a back four of Paul Parker, Steve Bruce, Gary Pallister and Denis Irwin; the trickery of Ryan Giggs and Andrei Kanchelskis on the wings, the presence of Roy Keane and Paul Ince in midfield, and the invention, flair and goals of Eric Cantona and Mark Hughes up front.

"The pace and power of this team was impossible to beat," said Bruce. "If you wanted to fight, we could fight you; if you wanted to play football, we could do that. We had pace, commitment, hunger, drive and limitless energy. For me, of course, I am a little biased, but I think it was as good a side as United have ever had."

The only blemishes on this historic season were missing out on becoming the first English side to win a domestic treble by losing to

---

"WE HAD PACE, COMMITMENT, HUNGER, DRIVE AND LIMITLESS ENERGY... IT WAS AS GOOD A SIDE AS UNITED HAVE EVER HAD"

Below
Manchester United celebrate winning the double after a 4-0 triumph over Chelsea in the 1994 FA Cup Final

Aston Villa in the League Cup final and making little impact in the European Cup.

During the season, United set a club record for most wins (41) and their longest-ever unbeaten run of 34 games in all competitions, as they comfortably defended their league title and finished with 92 points, eight ahead of Blackburn in second place. In the FA Cup final, United overcame Chelsea, who had earlier beaten them twice in the league that season, with a 4-0 victory featuring two penalties from Eric Cantona and goals from Ince and Hughes.

"Liberated from the pressures that quarter of a century without a title had imposed, our players brought a new authority to their game [in this season] and began to justify being rated as one of the best teams to wear United colours," a proud Ferguson has said.

The following 1994–95 season proved to be one of the most dramatic, chaotic and adrenaline-fuelled campaigns in United's entire history, full of soaring highs and desperate, unprecedented lows.

United's ambition had been to win a third successive title for the first time in their history and make a meaningful impact on the newly minted Champions League, but they would achieve neither.

In Europe, United were unable to get themselves out of the group stage, where they suffered a humiliating 4-0 defeat to Barcelona in the Camp Nou, which Ferguson said delivered "a bitter lesson... Keeping the ball is the name of the game in Europe, and they just don't understand."

Back in the more comfortable environment of the Premier League, United's title defence came under serious threat from

Blackburn Rovers, who were managed by Kenny Dalglish, bankrolled by Jack Walker, and inspired by Alan Shearer's constant supply of goals.

Ferguson decided he needed more goals from his own side and in January 1995 broke the British transfer record to sign Andy Cole from Newcastle for a fee of £7 million, with Keith Gillespie moving to Tyneside in turn.

United would beat Blackburn 1-0 on Cole's debut with a dramatic late winner from Cantona to fill Ferguson with confidence that his side were destined to be champions again, but just three days later United's season would begin to spectacularly unravel.

During a difficult game against Crystal Palace at Selhurst Park, Cantona was shown a red card for aiming a kick at Richard Shaw. As the Frenchman walked back to the tunnel he took offence at a Palace fan shouting abuse at him and assaulted him with a flying kick and a punch. As Ferguson has reflected, "Eric took us to heaven with that wonderful goal to beat Blackburn... we were now taken to hell."

Cantona would not play for United for another eight months as he was subjected to his club's initial ban, an extension from the Football Association and a court case that handed him a two-week prison sentence, which on appeal was commuted to community service.

While United were denied their main inspiration, they now had a cause, and they would only lose twice in their final 16 league games without him, which included a record 9-0 victory over Ipswich Town at Old Trafford that featured five goals from Cole.

On the final weekend of the season, United were a point behind Blackburn, and knew if Dalglish's side failed to win at Liverpool they could steal away the title with a win against West Ham at Upton Park.

Blackburn would indeed stumble, losing 2-1 at Anfield, but United could not manage more than a 1-1 draw in

Above Eric Cantona at Croydon Crown Court in March 1995 after successfully appealing his prison sentence for kicking a Crystal Palace fan
Below Eric Cantona celebrates scoring against Chelsea in a 3-0 win for United in April 1993 on their way to winning the Premier League

"WE HAVE ENTERTAINED THIS SEASON... ANYONE WHO HAS WATCHED US THIS SEASON HAS HAD THEIR MONEY'S WORTH"

east London, where they laid siege to West Ham's goal in an increasingly frantic second half. One more goal would have made them champions, but it didn't come, and instead they finished a solitary point behind Blackburn.

Six days later, an emotionally and physically drained United were not able to overcome their intense disappointment and fell to a 1-0 defeat to Everton in the FA Cup final at Wembley.

"It's five years since we've won nothing," reflected Ferguson at the time. "Sometimes players forget what defeat is like. They know now. But we have entertained this season, we never shut up shop or wasted time. Anyone who has watched us this season has had their money's worth, and I'm proud to say that."

United still had a settled squad ready to win the title again, and so it came as a huge shock when Ferguson began to dismantle it in the summer with the sale of three important and popular players. United's best midfielder, Paul Ince, was sold to Inter Milan; Andrei Kanchelskis, top scorer with 15 goals in the previous season, left for Everton; and club legend Mark Hughes was sold to Chelsea.

"Ferguson was attempting to do something that football history has shown to be the most difficult of all tasks: completing a smooth

BRUCE DRAGS UNITED BACK FROM THE BRINK

Two late goals from United's captain Steve Bruce in a famous game against Sheffield Wednesday kept them on track to win the title

On Easter Saturday 1993, Manchester United were a point behind league leaders Aston Villa in the Premier League table with only six games remaining and painfully aware it was at this stage of the previous season when their campaign had imploded.

The visitors to Old Trafford on this day were a strong Sheffield Wednesday side who would reach the final of both the League Cup and FA Cup that season, and with 25 minutes remaining they took the lead with a penalty converted by John Sheridan.

"An eerie feeling engulfed Old Trafford, the crowd were getting anxious, and that began to affect us," former United captain Steve Bruce has recalled.

With only four minutes left, Bruce himself equalised with a looping header, but there were no celebrations; it wasn't enough, and United knew they still needed another goal.

Deep into an unusually long seven minutes of added time, caused by an injury to the referee, Gary Pallister swung over a cross for his centre-back partner Bruce to meet with another firm header to score one of the most important and famous goals in United's entire history.

"At that moment Old Trafford exploded; I have never heard such noise in a stadium," Bruce has said. "The tension and nerves that had consumed us evaporated and were replaced by relief and joy."

United were now top of the table and a point ahead of Villa, who had drawn that afternoon. "We knew we couldn't be beaten now and that wait of 26 years was nearly over," Bruce has said.

transition from one championship-winning side to another without any loss of momentum," Roy Keane has reflected. "He had the easy option to do nothing and buy [more] success, but he took the hard, risky option and placed his trust in the club's young players. He liked a punt, but this was less of a gamble to those of us within the club [who knew these players]."

Ferguson had let three established players leave to give an opportunity to a talented group of young players he had been nurturing within the club and who would come to be known as the 'Class of '92' after winning the FA Youth Cup that year.

He was convinced the rare talent of David Beckham, Paul Scholes, Nicky Butt, Gary Neville, Phil Neville and Ryan Giggs, who were already in the first team, would keep delivering United trophies.

Despite this young new side losing 3-1 to Aston Villa on the opening day of the season, a defeat that

Above Manchester United celebrate winning the Premier League in May 1993 to become champions of England for the first time in 26 years
Below David Beckham celebrates scoring in United's 4-0 win over Newcastle in the 1996 Charity Shield at Wembley

prompted the former Liverpool captain Alan Hansen to dismiss them and claim on that evening's *Match Of The Day*, "You can't win anything with kids", United went on to lose only once more in their next 16 league games.

Bolstered by the return of Cantona in October, United grew in confidence and began to compete with Kevin Keegan's entertaining Newcastle side for the title, who at one stage held a 12-point lead in the Premier League.

In March 1996, United's 1-0 victory over Newcastle at St James' Park would prove to be a turning point, one that would drive them towards regaining the title, which they secured on the final day of the season with an impressive 3-0 victory over Middlesbrough at the Riverside Stadium.

United also made a third consecutive appearance in the FA Cup final, where they met Liverpool in a taut and tense game that was settled with only four minutes remaining when Cantona scored his 19th and final goal of the season.

"We had won another double," Keane, United's man of the match in the final, has said. "The moment of victory is short, but what's worth savouring is the vindication. The double vindicated the manager [because] he had won something with 'kids'."

After winning three titles in four seasons, the priority for the 1996-97 season was to win the club's first European Cup for three decades, but United would have to be content with making the semi-finals for the first time since 1969, where they lost 2-0 over two legs to the eventual winners Borussia Dortmund.

But in the Premier League normal service continued with yet another league title as they finished seven points ahead of second-placed Newcastle, Ferguson's young side visibly gaining in confidence, with Beckham winning that season's PFA Young Player of the Year and emerging as a real force at Old Trafford.

On the day United lifted the Premier League trophy Cantona appeared a little distracted, and within days he would announce his shock retirement from the game just before his 31st birthday.

In the following season, without the Frenchman, the catalyst for their Premier League success, as well as his successor as captain Roy Keane, who would miss almost the entire campaign after a serious injury in September, United would at first continue to prosper, and by March they had amassed a 12-point lead in the Premier League and reached the Champions League quarter-finals. But the loss of so much experience would begin to be felt by what was still a relatively young side as they lost to Monaco on away goals in Europe and could do nothing to stop a revived and powerful Arsenal side, in Arsène Wenger's first full season, overtaking them in the table with ten consecutive league wins.

Beaten but unbowed, Ferguson would spend the summer of 1998 rejuvenating his side with some key buys in anticipation of another gruelling season. Little could he have known how fruitful his efforts would be.

THE IMPOSSIBLE

DREAM

The treble couldn't be done. It was just too much to ask of any club... except Manchester United

Words Rob Clark

"**H**ey Yorkie, 27 games left – 27 more wins, we've had an unbelievable season." It started as a light-hearted moment when Peter Schmeichel said that to Dwight Yorke after the FA Cup fourth-round win over Liverpool. "It became our joke," said the great Dane. "Hey Yorkie, 26 games left – 26 more wins and we've had an unbelievable season..." The it gets below 10 wins and suddenly you're "Wait a minute...".

It all began in the summer of 1998. The previous season a home defeat by Arsenal in March followed by successive 1-1 draws at Old Trafford against Newcastle United and Liverpool in April had cost Manchester United the league title by a single point. Alex Ferguson decided, as ever, to refresh his squad and signed Jaap Stam from PSV Eindhoven (as pretty much a direct replacement for the departing Gary Pallister), Swedish winger Jesper Blomqvist from Parma and Dwight Yorke from Aston Villa. Villa hadn't wanted to sell Yorke, but the player pushed through a move. Ferguson always had in mind an ideal model of four top strikers that he could rotate and rest as necessary; now he had that.

Yorke brought goals galore, as expected, but more than that he brought an unforgettable smile and a bubbly, infectious personality that seemed to give the whole squad a lift after the narrow disappointment of the previous season. David Gill, who at the time was the finance director and later became one of the club's classiest and most astute chief executives, said, "At Manchester United, [transfer business] is mostly about buying new players. We're not a selling club. The profile of Manchester United is such that every time there's a rumour about a top player considering a move, we are bound to be mentioned. I'd be concerned if we weren't involved because it sends a message about the best clubs and their position in football."

Despite Ferguson's acquisitions the 1998–99 season didn't start in a particularly promising way – August saw draws with Leicester City and West Ham United, while September brought a heavy 3-0 defeat at Arsenal, which must have revived memories of the London club's double over United the previous season. Defeats by mid-table Sheffield Wednesday (November) and Middlesbrough (at home in December) did little to restore confidence, though in Europe United were engaged in some fabulous matches.

Drawn in a tough-looking group with Bayern Munich and Barcelona, United enjoyed two 3-3 draws with the Spanish giants. The first game saw two Barça penalties, a red card for Nicky Butt and a spectacular free kick from David Beckham. In the second game, Barcelona, fielding an 18-year-old Xavi in midfield, went ahead in the first minute, but United got themselves into the game and goals from Yorke (2) and Cole – working a superb one-two with Yorke – meant a hard-fought Nou Camp draw.

Those results were sufficient to end Barcelona's interest in the tournament before the final round of group matches, as they lost both home and away to Bayern Munich. They didn't assure United's progress, however, as in those days only the group winners were guaranteed a place in the knockouts and United finished

Above right Strikers supreme: Cole and Yorke parade the Premier League trophy around Old Trafford **Right** A sea of United fans come out to celebrate the treble winning bus parade **Below** Ole Gunnar Solskjaer scores the late, late winner in the Champions League final **Bottom left** A beaming Paul Scholes is embraced by Teddy Sheringham after scoring United's second goal in the FA Cup final

a point behind Bayern Munich having drawn at home and lost 2-1 away; fortunately, however, they went through as one of the two best-placed runners-up.

December brought elimination from the League Cup at the hands of Spurs, but after the turn of the year United embarked on an unbeaten run that took in 13 wins and five draws in the league and an FA Cup campaign in which they beat Middlesbrough, Liverpool, Fulham, Chelsea and Arsenal. In the middle came the 8-1 thrashing of Nottingham Forest at the City Ground, when Ole Gunnar Solskjaer, on as a 72nd-minute substitute for Yorke, scored four times in 18 minutes. The baby-faced assassin, as he was known, had earned the soubriquet 'super sub' in the 2-1 FA Cup fourth-round win over Liverpool. Trailing for much of the match to an early Michael Owen goal, United had battered their old foes, twice hitting a post, but couldn't find the breakthrough. In a mirror image of an even more important game later in the season, two minutes from time Yorke got the equaliser, and seconds later Solskjaer picked the ball out of

"THERE WAS TALK ABOUT [WINNING ALL THREE TROPHIES] BUT IT WAS STRICTLY BANTER. I DON'T THINK ANY OF US REALLY BELIEVED IT UNTIL WE GOT TO BARCELONA"

GIGGS' GLORY

It took one of the best solo goals of all time to keep the dream alive

The FA Cup semi-final against Arsenal had finished 0-0, so in the days of replays that meant reconvening at Villa Park a few days later. It was a replay that United largely dominated, with David Beckham scoring a fabulous goal after 17 minutes, but they couldn't put the game to bed and a fluke deflection from a Dennis Bergkamp shot brought the Gunners level. Suddenly, the tide seemed to be turning. Roy Keane was sent off for a second yellow, then a last-minute penalty was rightly awarded to Arsenal. Peter Schmeichel, however, spread his huge frame to keep out Bergkamp's effort (Arsenal's regular penalty taker, Bergkamp never took another spot kick for Arsenal). The game then went into extra time. With 109 minutes on the clock, Ryan Giggs intercepted a weary-looking crossfield pass from Patrick Vieira inside his own half. Weaving this way and that, turning the Arsenal defence inside out, Giggs beat four men before smashing an unstoppable shot past England goalkeeper David Seaman. It's probably the best FA Cup goal in history, and it kept United believing. "There were so many big games that spring," Beckham would later reflect, "but one stands out above the rest, the one that made everything possible."

Scholes' feet, switched feet himself and slotted it home. He had been on the pitch for nine minutes and those were his only two touches of the ball. The league win over Forest showcased Solskjaer's ability to read the play from the bench, come on late in a game, and immediately pick up the pace.

The league campaign remained a battle throughout though, with defending champions Arsenal refusing to give up or be shaken off. From mid-December onwards, Arsenal played 27 games and the only one they lost was the FA Cup semi-final replay (see above).

On the final day of the league season, United were home to Spurs while Arsenal hosted Aston Villa, both teams in the top half of the table but with little to play for themselves except pride. Despite battering Spurs throughout, United went behind to a Les Ferdinand goal, but superb strikes from Beckham and Cole put them 2-1 up and Spurs had no answer. It was then a case of seeing out the rest of the game with the minimum of fuss. It was the first time that United had won the Premier League in front of their own fans, and they did it in what would proved to be Schmeichel's last game at Old Trafford. Yet the celebrations were joyous but restrained in light of the two cup finals still to come.

The FA Cup had already provided some heart-stopping moments, including the late, late turnaround against Liverpool, a six-round replay victory over Chelsea at Stamford Bridge and the dramatic semi-final replay win over Arsenal. The final itself was, in truth, an anti-climax. Newcastle United just weren't able to really threaten the United goal at all; they had plenty of possession but few chances, while United were clinical in their execution. "It was so easy for us," Schmeichel said dismissively. "Even at 1-0 we started conserving energy for the next game."

Images Getty Images

The Geordies never appeared capable of causing an upset. Even captain Roy Keane going off after a couple of minutes didn't ruffle United's composure – they simply brought on Teddy Sheringham and on 11 minutes the England striker put his team ahead. When Scholes got the second, from a lovely lay-off by Sheringham, on 53 minutes, the game was well and truly over. Even the genius of manager Ruud Gullit couldn't inspire Newcastle to respond. No manager had ever led his team to two English league and cup doubles before; Ferguson had now done this on three separate occasions, making him the most successful manager of all time.

And so to Europe. Inter Milan were up first in the quarter-final first leg at Old Trafford, and United produced a strong performance, with Beckham in particular causing havoc down the right flank and laying on two first-half goals for Yorke. The second leg saw a solid defensive effort in which United conceded only a 63rd-minute goal and suffered few other alarms. A late close-range equaliser from Scholes meant it was 1-1 on the night and 3-1 to United on aggregate.

But that wasn't the end of the Italian threat. The epic semi-final matches against Juventus (see page 85) were only just navigated to set up a third meeting of the season with Bayern Munich. All of a sudden Schmeichel and Yorke's jokey exchange had become deadly serious. "At no stage until after the FA Cup final did we really think we could win all three trophies," said Cole. "There was talk about it among the lads but it was strictly banter.
I don't think any of us really believed it until we got to Barcelona."

The final turned out to be a disappointing match, all told. It was scrappy throughout and very stop-start. "We just couldn't get into the game," said Yorke. "It was so patchy and for some reason we just never got three or four passes together."

A fifth-minute free kick from Mario Basler gave the Germans the lead, and United had few clear-cut opportunities to get back into the game. In the second half it was Bayern who had the better chances,

"WE'D HARDLY HAD TIME TO DRAW BREATH WHEN THERE WAS ANOTHER GOAL"

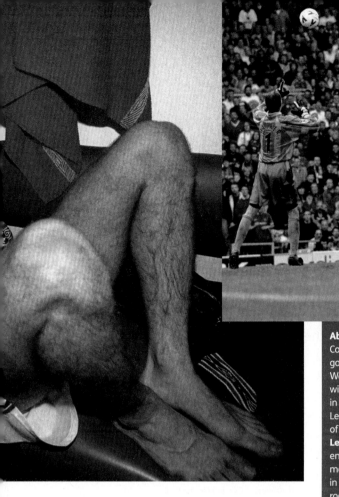

There were 93 minutes on the clock when United were given yet another corner. This time Sheringham turned provider, knocking the ball towards the far post, where Solskjaer instinctively stuck out a leg to redirect the ball and turned it high into the net. "Manchester United have reached the Promised Land!" announced Tyldsley during the match. "Nobody will ever win a European Cup final more dramatically than this!"

Later he reflected on those incredible final three minutes. "We'd hardly had time to draw breath, me and Ron Atkinson in the commentary box, when there was another goal. My lasting memory of that night is the faces of the Bayern Munich players; they looked like victims of a disaster. It's an overused word in a football context, but we'd never really seen a German team in that state before."

All this was happening while UEFA President Lennart Johansson was making his way down to pitchside for the presentation. Because he was using an internal lift he had no idea what was transpiring until he got there. "I was confused," he said. "It cannot be, the winners are crying and the losers are dancing."

"United played excellent attacking football in those last minutes," said Bayern and Germany captain Lothar Matthäus graciously after being substituted before the great comeback. "They had nothing to lose and we just tried to protect our result, which was surely a mistake. You have to congratulate United." Ferguson was more succinct in his appraisal. "Football! Bloody hell!"

Winning the treble was an impossible dream. Until it wasn't. And after the pain of the Munich air disaster and the long wait for a second European Cup, it was fitting that United should be the club to achieve it. They remain the only English club to do so. And long after the partying was over, Sir Alex Ferguson summed it up perfectly: "The celebrations begun by that goal will never really stop."

Above Andy Cole lobs Spurs goalkeeper Ian Walker for the winning goal in the final League match of the season
Left Becks enjoys a brief moment alone in the dressing room with the FA Cup
Far left top The imperious Jaap Stam was a vital link in the United defence
Far left bottom A delighted Alex Ferguson holds the ultimate prize close

including a Mehmet Scholl chip that bounced off the post and back into Schmeichel's arms and a Carsten Jancker overhead effort that cannoned off the crossbar. "Can United score?" asked commentator Clive Tyldsley. "They always score." Prophetic words.

With time running out, United were awarded a 90th-minute corner. Schmeichel came up to throw some doubt into German minds. Maybe it distracted the defence; certainly it seemed as if Yorke had a little more room at the back post when he nodded Beckham's cross into the middle of the area. The ball fell to Ryan Giggs, who helped it on to Sheringham, the former Spurs striker poking home to bring United level. "Name on the trophy!" yelled Tyldsley. On the sidelines Assistant Manager Steve McLaren was preparing for extra time. "Sit down, Steve," his boss told him. "This match isn't over yet."

KEANE TURNS IT AROUND
The United stunned Juve to reach Champions League final

Juventus. An iconic name in world sport and the sizeable obstacle barring United's way to the Champions League final in '99. Managed by Carlo Ancelotti and boasting talents such as Zinedine Zidane and Didier Deschamps from France's World Cup-winning side of 1998, plus Dutch midfield giant Edgar Davids and prolific Italian striker Filippo Inzaghi, Juve were a dangerous side. After a 1-1 draw in Manchester they were the favourites, and even more so after 15 minutes of the second leg in Turin, when Inzaghi put them 2-0 up. Then came Roy Keane. He dragged United back into the contest, scoring on 24 minutes, then through sheer will power and personality he drove his team forward, dominating the midfield. Yorke equalised before half-time and, as they continued to press, United's pace and aggression overran the Italians. They hit the woodwork twice before Cole wrapped up the game with a late winner. But victory came at a cost: both Keane and Paul Scholes got bookings that ruled them out of the final. Keane said later that he was so wrapped up in the game that the consequences of his yellow card barely registered at the time. No doubt Ferguson was already plotting how he would cope without his first-choice central midfield in the final.

Images Getty Images

DOMESTIC DOMINATION
IN THE NEW MILLENNIUM

Manchester United started the new millennium as Premier League champions, and after a three-year dip roared back to the top of the table

Words Sam Pilger

I n the summer of 1999 I met with Sir Alex Ferguson in his office at The Cliff training ground, days before his players reported back for the new season.

At the end of the previous campaign United had become the first English club to win the treble of the Premier League, the FA Cup and the Champions League. But the United manager, who had recently been knighted, was not interested in basking in the glory of these unprecedented achievements with me; rather, he was already making plans to win everything all over again.

"Before the last champagne bubble had popped at our Barcelona celebrations, some people were ready to point out that my competitive edge was sure to be terminally blunted by winning the treble," Ferguson would later say. "I never for a moment saw the European Cup as the final summit. Having won it, why shouldn't we win it again? Having made ourselves club champions of our own continent, why shouldn't we set out to become champions of the world as well?"

Ferguson accomplished this in November 1999 when United became the first British side to become world champions with a 1-0 victory over the Brazilian side Palmeiras in the Intercontinental Cup in Tokyo, Japan.

Two months later United had another opportunity to claim this title in the inaugural FIFA Club World Cup in Brazil, which they were

Top right
Ronaldo and Rooney in action against AC Milan
Right
Champions again in 2003
Below right
Van Nistelrooy celebrates scoring including against Newcastle in the 2005 FA Cup semi-final
Below
A beaming Ronaldo sports his winners medal in 2007

forced to withdraw from the FA Cup to compete in, but they failed to progress beyond the group stage.

Back in the Premier League, United strolled to another title that season, finishing 18 points ahead of second-placed Arsenal, although they were unable to defend their European title, losing 3-2 on aggregate to Real Madrid in the quarter-finals.

The following season, Ferguson became the most successful manager in English football as United finished a comfortable ten points ahead of Arsenal in the table.

With the French World Cup winner Fabien Barthez now in goal and a 35-year-old Teddy Sheringham scoring 21 goals and winning the Footballer of the Year award, United were too good for their nearest rivals Arsenal, which they comprehensively proved by beating them 6-1 at Old Trafford in February 2001.

However, United could not translate this domestic dominance into more European success and were stopped again in the Champions League quarter-finals, losing 3-1 over two legs to the eventual winners Bayern Munich.

The morning after the first leg of this tie I met with the United captain Roy Keane, who was already fearing the worst. "We really have to be careful to think that our success is going to go on and on. We really have to start dominating Europe as well as the Premiership. Sometimes you don't realise it, maybe it's already

coming to the end. All good things come to an end. I'm not being over-dramatic, but if we don't win the European Cup this year then there will be changes."

Keane was proved right that summer. Ferguson twice broke the British transfer record to sign the Dutch striker Ruud van Nistelrooy from PSV Eindhoven for £19 million and the Argentinian midfielder Juan Sebastián Verón from Lazio for £28.1 million.

However, United's momentum was somewhat slowed by Ferguson's surprising decision – which he would later admit was a "mistake" – to also sell his best defender, Jaap Stam, to Lazio and buy 35-year-old French defender Laurent Blanc from Inter Milan.

While Van Nistelrooy scored 36 goals during the 2001–02 season, Verón and Blanc initially struggled, and United's defence suddenly appeared fragile, as they lost nine league games to finish third in the table and surrender their title to Arsenal, who became champions with a 1-0 win at Old Trafford in May.

At the start of the 2002–03 season, the jubilant Arsenal manager Arsène Wenger had claimed "a shift of power" was happening in the Premier League, but nine months later United reclaimed the title, their fourth in five years. In March 2003, Arsenal had been on course to successfully defend their title with an eight-point lead over United in the table, but Ferguson's side, partially stung by losing the League Cup final to Liverpool in the same month, completed an incredible run of 18 unbeaten Premier League games to overtake them and reclaim the title.

The brilliance of Rio Ferdinand in the centre of defence, who had been signed a year earlier from Leeds, and the goals of Van Nistelrooy, who scored a total of 44 that season, were major factors in United's revival.

"This is the sweetest one, without doubt," Ferguson said at the time. "It has been an heroic achievement by the players and everyone at the club, simply because of the lead Arsenal had and all the triumphant talk that the title was theirs."

The following season, Arsenal responded by going through the 2003–04 Premier League season unbeaten to claim both the trophy and the title of 'The Invincibles', while United had to be content with beating them in the FA Cup semi-final at Villa Park before overcoming Millwall 3-0 in the final in Cardiff.

In the summer of 2004, the arrival of José Mourinho – who called himself 'The Special One' – at Chelsea, fresh from winning the Champions League with Porto, would present both Arsenal and United with a new challenge, and they were soon placed in his shadow as he won consecutive Premier League titles in 2005 and 2006.

During these years Ferguson was rebuilding a new side, adding 18-year-old Cristiano Ronaldo from Sporting Lisbon for £12.4 million (then a world-record transfer fee for a teenager) in 2003, and a year later, 18-year-old Wayne Rooney from Everton for £27 million, the experienced goalkeeper Edwin van der Sar in 2005, and in January 2006, two new defenders, Patrice Evra and Nemanja Vidić.

In 2004–05 United endured a rare trophyless season, losing an FA Cup final to Arsenal they had dominated, but in the following season they won the League Cup with a 4-0 victory over Wigan Athletic in Cardiff in February 2006.

After three seasons without winning the title, United were now ready to challenge Chelsea, and they finally overhauled them in 2006–07, finishing six points clear at the top of the table.

"It was a great feeling winning the title for the first time since 2002–03, claiming it back after all the doubts," Gary Neville has since reflected. "There had been calls for the manager to quit. There were times, even in the dressing room, we wondered if long-term decline had set in. Chelsea had spent all the money, they had looked so dominant, so we had a massive celebration that we were back on top."

United had been inspired to the title by the emerging talent of Ronaldo, who that season was transformed from a promising youngster into one of the best players in the world, scoring 23 goals and being voted the Footballer of the Year.

"We were champions mostly thanks to Ronaldo," Neville has said. "The way he carried us in 2006–07 marks it as his best season. I felt I owed him my championship medal."

BEST OF
ENEMIES

Arsène Wenger and Sir Alex Ferguson
shaped the Premier League with their
teams, but their rivalry was just as defining

Words Mark White

A

rsène Wenger took to the Emirates Stadium pitch for the last time in 2018 following a 5-0 victory against Burnley. The legendary manager was leaving the club he loved, and for one final time he addressed the fans who had followed him for 22 years.

One of the first cheers in Wenger's speech, however, came for the man with whom the Frenchman had formed the Premier League's defining rivalry: Sir Alex Ferguson. Ferguson was recovering from a brain haemorrhage he'd suffered earlier that month, and with all eyes on Wenger, one of the first things he asked from the crowd was to wish Ferguson – a man who Gunners knew almost intimately well – the best of health.

By this point, the rivalry was long in the past. Time had thawed the ice between two bitter opponents, warming it into mutual respect and even appreciation for what the other had achieved. Now, reportedly, the pair are friends. They discuss football over a glass of wine. But it wasn't always that way.

ARSÈNE WHO?

Gunners fans wondered whether they were set to get Johan Cruyff as their manager in 1996. Instead, vice-chairman David Dein was instrumental in recommending a friend of his with whom he'd sung karaoke one night in the late 1980s.

"They say he's an intelligent man, right? Speaks five languages?" Ferguson said to the media after Wenger's appointment. "I've got a 15-year-old boy from the Ivory Coast who speaks five languages."

It's safe to say that the Scotsman was not fearful of being usurped as the king of English football. After all, he had no equal.

Fergie was offered the Arsenal job in 1986 but chose to manage Scotland at the World Cup before taking charge of United after the tournament. His early years in the job were tough, but the Old Trafford outfit kept the faith and were eventually repaid when shrewd signings started to blossom.

Above Arsène Wenger is unveiled to the press at Highbury in 1996
Below Sir Alex Ferguson addresses reporters at United's Carrington training ground ahead of a clash with Arsenal during the 2005-06 season

By 1996, United had won three of the first four Premier League campaigns and completed a domestic double in two, helped in no small part by the schemes and mind games their manager deployed. In 1992 Ferguson had outwitted Howard Wilkinson of Leeds United to turn an enquiry for Denis Irwin into the catalytic capture of Eric Cantona. He then followed this superb trick by hoodwinking Blackburn Rovers boss Kenny Dalglish to sign Roy Keane behind his back in 1993, sending his countryman into a seething rage. And Fergie was at it again just months before Wenger came to the Premier League, provoking Newcastle United manager Kevin Keegan to such an extent that he spiralled into his now iconic "I would love it" rant in response to Ferguson's snipes. It was lonely at the top for the United gaffer – and that's exactly how he liked it.

In truth, Wenger wasn't Ferguson's challenger immediately. The Frenchman began his revolution during the 1996-97 season by revitalising an ageing defence, changing the dietary habits of his players and bringing more little-known gems through Highbury's famous Marble Halls. Patrick Vieira was the first, with Emmanuel Petit and Nicolas Anelka following. The classic back four was given a new lease of life, and it wasn't just the drinking culture of the

previous regime that disappeared: you weren't even allowed sugar in your tea.

"He's a novice. He should keep his opinions to Japanese football," Fergie laughed when Wenger questioned the fixture scheduling favouring United that year. He'd have no doubt scoffed at the marginal gains in diet and fitness Wenger was making while his side strolled to a fourth title. He wasn't laughing in Wenger's second season, though.

Having lost 3-0 to Derby County the previous week, Arsenal were in danger of handing United a seven-point lead at the top of the Premier League table in November 1997 when they hosted a Reds Devils side who were sweeping all before them. The match would prove to be the first of many dramatic clashes between the two managers, with Arsenal racing into a 2-0 lead before Teddy Sheringham pulled the visitors level with a brace before half-time. In the end, former United trainee David Platt's late goal won the game. Yet while it was first blood to Wenger, by the second half of the season United were 11 points up, with Arsenal constantly chasing.

The 1997–98 title was to be decided as much by nerve as talent. The bottle that United had shown for years had to be matched by Arsenal; the mind games that Keegan had succumbed to had to be ignored. In March 1998, Arsenal showed

BATTLE OF OLD TRAFFORD

An enraged Arsenal delighted in tormenting van Nistelrooy after a crucial miss in a fiery 2003 encounter

"I can't think of any other word when I was getting ready to do battle with Arsenal: hatred was the word," cantankerous Corkonian Roy Keane claimed of United's fiercest title rivals. "But I behaved myself that day and I regret it."

In truth, he was one of few who did. But though Lauren, Martin Keown, Patrick Vieira and Ray Parlour were all suspended by the FA, the game that would come to be known as the Battle of Old Trafford was a turning point in the Gunners' 2003–04 season.

Despite being unbeaten up to that point, Arsenal were yet to truly slide into fifth gear, but after surviving a stoppage-time penalty to secure a 0-0 draw at United, Wenger's men defeated Newcastle, Liverpool and Chelsea, before wins over Leeds and Tottenham put them in the driving seat for the title. That match at Old Trafford was the closest that the Gunners came to defeat all season, and following the fiery confrontations at full-time they were a team reborn.

"We could have paid for a new roof at the FA for the amount we paid in fines, but I don't go through my life regretting things," Keown later claimed. "You could say what we did was unforgivable, but we jumped up and down around him. The media were focusing on that rather than the result.

"I rang my wife after the game, and she's usually very supportive, but she said 'I think you've gone and done it now.' It was the first time she'd ever said anything like that."

"ARSENAL DID THE DOUBLE OVER UNITED THAT SEASON"

their mettle, winning 1-0 at Old Trafford through a Marc Overmars goal.

"I told you last week that the race was not over when the bookmakers stopped betting," Wenger said as Manchester bookmaker Fred Done paid out £17,000 early on a United title win. "Surprise, surprise, they have started taking money again..."

Arsenal did the double over United that season as they secured both the league title and the FA Cup. The bookies wouldn't be so cocky in future. Neither would Ferguson.

A WAR OF WORDS

The following season, the pendulum would swing back to the North West, with the campaign on both sides hinging on a single penalty. Neck and neck in the title race, United and Arsenal met in the FA Cup semi-final. With just seconds of normal time to go, Phil Neville brought Ray Parlour down inside the United box. Referee David Elleray blew for a spot-kick, and up stepped Dennis

Top Marc Overmars nets a crucial winner at Old Trafford
Above Ferguson complains to an unmoved Wenger in 2004 at Highbury
Above right Arsenal players confront Ruud van Nistelrooy after the Dutchman's missed penalty at Old Trafford

Bergkamp – the Ice Man – to end United's treble dreams.

What happened next is perhaps the biggest sliding doors moment of Wenger's Arsenal career. The Dutchman missed, Peter Schmeichel pawing his effort away to keep United in the tie. Ryan Giggs' spectacular solo run would eventually snatch victory for United, a triumph that provided them with the mental push to snatch back the title en route to winning an unprecedented treble. Bergkamp never took a penalty for the Gunners again. Wenger chose to start rebuilding his tired side.

United made it three league titles in a row from 1999 to 2001, with memorable jabs from either side punctuating this period. Thierry Henry's iconic twist-and-flick finish at Highbury would sink United in 2000; United would respond with a 6-1 thumping in the reverse tie.

By the summer of 2001, however, Arsenal were ready to compete again – and in November, again, Arsenal defeated United at Highbury. If two mistakes and a wry smile from Fabien Barthez didn't leave Ferguson close to exploding, then perhaps Wenger's slightly condescending comment about enjoying Ferguson keeping him "on his toes" the following February would, as the Scotsman U-turned on his retirement plans.

Arsenal were an unstoppable force that season, playing with flair and confidence. The Gunners scored in every match that season, were unbeaten away and managed a clean sweep of the Golden Boot (Thierry Henry), Football Writers' Association Footballer of the Year (Robert Pires), Barclaycard Player of the Year (Freddie Ljungberg) and Barclaycard Manager of the Year (Wenger, of course).

The fickle hand of fate decided that a trip to Old Trafford, just before the FA Cup final, would decide the title. Incredibly, Wenger left Henry and Bergkamp out and was rewarded with a magnificent masterclass from Ray Parlour, as Sylvain Wiltord's solitary goal snatched the title back from the Red Devils. Ferguson was especially livid.

"He never comes for a drink with the opposing manager after matches," he claimed of his opposite number. "He's the only manager in the Premiership not to do so. It is a tradition here. It would be good for him to accept the tradition."

Wenger, meanwhile, could well have been too busy partying in Fergie's own stadium to care. But that wasn't all Ferguson had to say on the matter when he called the new Premier League champions "scrappers who rely on belligerence".

Wenger smiled at this comment, his Gallic grin preceding the words, "Everyone thinks they have the prettiest wife at home."

Little did he perhaps know that he had truly made it personal. The rivalry was ready to boil over, with Sir Alex believing the quip had been aimed at his wife Cathy. Unbelievably, the war between the two clubs was only just beginning.

FINES AND FOOD FIGHTS

Just as in 1998–99, the 2002–03 title was lost by Arsenal as much as it was won by United. The Gunners began the season on an unbeaten quest, compliments thrown their way like confetti, and fittingly it was a future United talisman, Wayne Rooney, who delivered their first defeat of six in the league that helped to pass the silver handles back to Roy Keane's grateful grasp.

And United took as much pleasure in their rivals' downfall as they did their own victory. December saw a 2-0 home win at Old Trafford, with Wenger complaining of a handball, while an FA Cup fifth-round tie brought tensions back to the boil early.

Wenger's 'scrappers' travelled to Old Trafford to find the most physical test they'd faced all season. Two minutes in, Paul Scholes had slammed into the back of Patrick Vieira, with all but two players crowding around each other; a minute later, Ruud van Nistelrooy charged into Martin Keown at thigh height. Miraculously, no one was sent off as Arsenal kept their heads to win 2-0, but in the aftermath Ferguson famously kicked a boot in the dressing room that connected with David Beckham's eyebrow.

This was just one of many high-tension matches between Arsenal and United. Sol Campbell was sent off in the 2-2 draw at Highbury that effectively ended Arsenal's chances of winning the league, before a frosty Charity Shield on a baking-hot day at the Millennium Stadium in August was won by United on penalties.

In September 2003, tempers truly spilt over in what was later known as 'The Battle of Old Trafford'. Unlike the FA Cup clash the previous season, it took longer to explode.

In fact, the match was fairly uneventful until Patrick Vieira was given a second yellow card ten minutes from time. Van Nistelrooy

clattered into Vieira, provoking a kick out from the Frenchman, who was dismissed; both teams swarmed the referee, with goalkeeper Jens Lehmann pointing at van Nistelrooy as United players dragged the Dutchman away from the melee, while Keane and Vieira came close to blows in the centre of it all. It erupted again minutes later when Keown was judged to have brought Diego Forlán down in the penalty area in stoppage time. Van Nistelrooy stepped up to take the resulting spot-kick, and when the ball ricocheted off the bar and full-time was blown the Arsenal players

Above Captains Keane and Vieira regularly came to blows
Right Wenger and Ferguson in the aftermath of United's 2-0 win at Old Trafford in 2004, a result that ended Arsenal's 49-match unbeaten run

THE RIVALRY IN QUOTES

"He's at a big club – well, Arsenal used to be a big club – and maybe next year he could be in the same situation. I wonder what his story will be then."
FERGUSON ON WENGER (1997)

"I enjoy our rivalry. It is good for Arsenal, good for Manchester United and good for both of us."
WENGER (2002)

"It's a disgrace, but I don't expect Wenger to ever apologise… he's that type of person."
FERGUSON ON PIZZAGATE (2004)

"He has lost all sense of reality. He is going out looking for a confrontation, then asking the person he is confronting to apologise."
WENGER ON FERGUSON (2004)

THE ICE THAWS

With Arsenal moving into a new stadium and Ferguson still competing at the top, the pair's rivalry never again reached the animosity of 'Pizzagate'. Games between the two were no longer title deciders either.

In 2007, Arsenal would turn a 1-0 deficit into a 2-1 win at the Emirates to make the new ground feel like home for the first time, while two years later, Wenger would be sent to the Old Trafford stands, arms outstretched, in an iconic Premier League image. By this point, there was enough water under the bridge, and when United knocked Wenger's young guns out of the Champions League semi-finals, the pair shook hands as rivals but no longer sworn enemies; Ferguson even suggested that the two old masters of English football could ride out into the sunset together at the end of their careers.

Ultimately, it was a change in status that changed the relationship. Ferguson retired at the top, while Wenger's job readjusted to staying in the top four. Both recognised this.

"It's unfair, the criticism of the man," Ferguson would claim in the aftermath of 2011's 8-2 mauling of Arsenal, perhaps the moment that signalled the end of the pair standing as equals in terms of the Premier League. Arsenal would even sell Robin van Persie to United in 2012: once unthinkable, but Arsenal were not in the shape to be troubling the Red Devils.

When Wenger left management in 2018, it was Ferguson who led the tributes, presenting Wenger with a gift at the Frenchman's final trip to Old Trafford.

"He is, without doubt, one of the greatest Premier League managers and I am proud to have been a rival, a colleague and a friend to such a great man," Ferguson announced.

After all, Wenger was the only man who could truly challenge him for so long. It was lonely at the top before him – and then the pair shared a unique, intense rivalry that would provide some of the most talked-about moments English football has ever known.

surrounded the Dutchman. Keown infamously jumped over the United striker as Lauren and Parlour looked to antagonise. Ashley Cole squared up to Cristiano Ronaldo and Lauren faced off with Ryan Giggs as coaching staff pulled the players apart.

Six Arsenal players, two United players and Arsenal as a club were charged with improper conduct by the FA. The Gunners were slapped with a £175,000 fine as players on both sides were sanctioned.

"In a ferocious game, I think my players behaved properly," Ferguson said after. Perhaps neither of the two managers could honestly defend their players a year later.

Wenger had the bragging rights in 2003–04, leading Arsenal to an unbeaten title, though Ferguson knocked Arsenal out of an FA Cup semi-final once more. Naturally, game no.50 of Arsenal's long unbeaten run was scheduled for Old Trafford. Greater Manchester Police spoke to referee Mike Riley about the importance of the players

remaining under control, but what should have been a spectacle of football rapidly descended into a storm of tackles.

Rio Ferdinand could have been sent off early, while Gary Neville and van Nistelrooy were lucky not to be cautioned or worse. When Wayne Rooney won a second-half penalty the Gunners were enraged.

This time, Arsenal kept their tempers to the tunnel. Campbell refused to shake Rooney's hand as pizza was thrown by Cesc Fàbregas at Ferguson. An incensed Henry had to be restrained, with Ferguson defending his players from Wenger. "What do you want to do about it?" Wenger asked in response. In the aftermath, Wenger would accuse van Nistelrooy of cheating, as well as criticising referee Riley.

"We can only master our own performance, not the referee's," the Frenchman would conclude. It was the last time that he and Ferguson would even be on speaking terms for almost five years.

Above Arsène Wenger is sent to the Old Trafford stands for kicking a bottle in 2009 **Below** Arsène Wenger and Sir Alex Ferguson meet one final time on the Old Trafford touchline in April 2018

"I'm ready to take the blame for all the problems of English football if that is what he wants."

WENGER, IN REACTION TO COMMENTS MADE BY SIR ALEX FERGUSON, WHO HIGHLIGHTED THE LACK OF HOMEGROWN PLAYERS AT ARSENAL (2007)

"I won 13 leagues but I was never near going through a season undefeated. The achievement stands above everything else, and it was Arsène's."
FERGUSON (2021)

TEN YEARS OF THE GLAZERS AT MANCHESTER UNITED

GLAZER

The Glazers have held the reins of power at Old Trafford for almost 18 years. We assess the impact of their first decade in charge, why their ownership is so controversial, and why it may soon end

Words Jonathan Fadugba

The story of Malcolm Glazer at Manchester United is one laced with contradiction. Here was an intensely private man who fought tooth and nail to own one of sport's biggest, most high-profile brands. A man with a net worth of $4.4 billion who continued to buy his trousers for $19.95, even taking pleasure in the fact. A man who irrevocably altered the history of Manchester United, reportedly without ever having set foot in Old Trafford. But who was Malcolm Glazer and how did he come to own one of the biggest football clubs on Earth?

Malcolm Glazer was born in 1928 in Rochester, New York, the son of Lithuanian immigrants. At the age of eight he went to work for his father's watch parts business, taking over and expanding the firm after his father died when he was 15. In the 1950s, Glazer quit Rochester's Sampson College after just six weeks. Fiercely driven, his goal was clear: set about building a business empire that would make as much money as possible. "All gamblers die broke" was a favourite saying of his. After leaving college, Glazer focused his energy on the jewellery business he'd been running in his spare time. He began to turn a profit, eventually expanding his portfolio by dipping into the property market, buying holiday homes and static

caravans in Rochester. Other business interests included food-service equipment, food packaging, food supplies, marine protein, broadcasting, healthcare, real estate, banking, natural gas and oil production, stocks, bonds and government securities. He had "an eye for value" according to business and finance bible *Forbes*. Such shrewd business acumen saw Glazer turn to sports franchise ownership in 1995, when he paid a then-record $192 million to buy the Tampa Bay Buccaneers. That they're today valued at $1.2 billion tells its own story. Under Glazer, the Bucs moved into a newly built stadium, opened a huge, state-of-the-art training facility and in 2002 won the Super Bowl for the first time in their history. But it wasn't all roses and coronations. While Glazer "turned this joke of a franchise into one of the most valuable commodities in sports", as *Tampa Bay Times* reporter John Romano put it, he earned a reputation as a hard-nosed, shadowy figure who alienated many. "He was an outsider who never sought our love and, subsequently, never gained our trust," said Romano.

The Manchester United takeover wasn't the only bitter struggle of Glazer's professional career. He fought his siblings for 12 years over the rights to his mother's

Below Arsenal fans gleefully mock United's new owners

estate after she died in 1980. And within weeks of taking over at Tampa Bay he threatened to up sticks and move the franchise if a new stadium wasn't built using taxpayers' money. "Glazer was a businessman, not a public servant," Romano notes. The stadium was paid for with public money to the tune of $194 million.

Judging by his prior dealings, there's every reason to believe that the principal motivation behind Glazer's purchase of United was profit.

A £790-million leveraged buyout plunged one of football's most profitable football clubs into a mountain of debt. But after the Red Devils announced a new sponsorship deal with Adidas, Wall Street afforded the club a market value of $3 billion – an incredible return on their investment should they ever sell up. According to Glazer's son Joel, who acts as club co-chairman with his brother Avram, the family have long been football fans. "I had a room-mate in college who was from London, and who to this day is still my best friend," he told MUTV after the takeover in 2005. "Every Saturday morning he'd be there with his little radio trying to pick up the Tottenham games.

It was infectious, and the more I learnt about the game over here the more passionate I got."

LET THE BIDDING BEGIN

In November 2022 the Glazers announced their intentions to sell United, but who can afford their asking price?

The Glazers' declaration of their intent to sell United in late 2022 felt like an early Christmas present for fans across the world. Finally, an end to their widely loathed ownership felt like a real possibility. And then they announced their valuation of the club: £6 billion, and not a penny less.

Financial experts believe United's true worth in the current economic climate is approximately £3.7 billion, a colossal fee but nowhere near what the Glazer family appear willing to accept. Chelsea, benefiting from the added advantage of being located in London, were sold for £2.5 billion in May 2022, and if United were to be purchased for £6 billion the deal would dwarf the £3.8 billion paid by the Walton-Penner group for the Denver Broncos in the summer of 2022, a record fee for a sports team at the time of writing.

Various potential suitors have been circulated in the press, from the Qatar Investment Authority (owners of PSG and able to draw on $450 billion) to Twitter owner Elon Musk (net worth $188 billion) and INEOS founder and CEO (not to mention lifelong United fan) Sir Jim Ratcliffe, valued at $28 billion.

If a full sale of the club cannot be agreed then an alternative could see the Glazers selling a share of the club and remaining at Old Trafford.

THE GLAZERS
DID IT TAINT FERGIE'S LEGACY?

NO

PETE MOLYNEUX

Season ticket holder and author of *Ta Ra Fergie*, having held up *that* banner in 1989

The fallout from Sir Alex Ferguson's row with [John] Magnier and [JP] McManus probably hastened the Glazer transaction. You'd have to admit the whole affair had an impact on the club and team.

You can't have a situation in any business where a senior manager is at loggerheads with the largest shareholder to the point where legal action is underway. It was a dangerous chapter in Manchester United's history. Ferguson was distracted – if you look at United's purchases in that time, Eric Djemba-Djemba, David Bellion, Alan Smith, Liam Miller and Kleberson weren't Manchester United calibre – but he was bound to be: he was battling for a stake of a multi-million-pound personal fortune. That stalled United's renaissance, but long-term, he fixed it on the field – as he always did.

I'd say it's been more that Ferguson 'saved' the Glazers than the Glazers saving Ferguson from Magnier and McManus. United's record once Fergie got the football back on track with the 2007 title took most of the real venom out of the anti-Glazer campaign. I don't feel Magnier and McManus would necessarily have made better owners than the Glazers, but they would have handled the early PR better. I didn't feel let down; nor do I believe Sir Alex sold out on his socialist roots. Without getting too deep, the big question is, how does a very successful person in business square the circle if they have socialism at their heart? His legacy at Old Trafford is his record of winning trophies, playing football the United way and putting my club right back where they belong – consistently challenging for domestic honours, taking on Europe's finest and aiming to rule the world! His time at Old Trafford had blemishes, but they were a small price to pay for the best 26 years any United supporter has enjoyed.

YES

COLIN HENDRIE

Vice-chairman, Independent Manchester United Supporters Association

The Magnier and McManus row was probably the last time Ferguson enjoyed the unequivocal support of the supporters. There were 'F**k Off Magnier' T-shirts, and Fergie's name was chanted around the ground to show our support for him. There's no doubt his fight with Magnier drew strength from this.

There were other protests as well: one at Hereford Racecourse, where John Magnier had horses running, and another planned for Cheltenham Gold Cup day, and those really seemed to put the wind up Magnier, as it was affecting his core business. Then Ferguson asked fans to call off the Cheltenham protest, saying it was "the equivalent of the FA Cup final to horse racing fans". He had settled with Magnier, for £2.5 million as it turns out. And there it was: the protests ended flatly. In my opinion, Ferguson had plainly used the fans for his own benefit, and that was the last time he could rely on us to support him without question.

The upshot of the whole falling-out was that Fergie was put on a one-year rolling contract – meaning there would be no big payout if he walked – and there's strong speculation that his role in transfers was reduced to saying "I want that one". If that was the case, it must have been painful for a man used to the old school ways of doing things, and therefore the change of ownership [to the Glazers] must have seemed like he was having his b****cks taken out of Magnier's vice. Did I feel let down by it all? Yes, of course. Ferguson was asked to support the fight against the Glazers' takeover of the club and as far as we were concerned, he chose to support them instead.

Overall, I would certainly say that the Glazer affair, and the way Ferguson dealt with it, ultimately tainted his legacy at Manchester United.

MONEY, MONEY, MONEY

With some £680m in debt repayments, bank charges and interest paid under
Glazer family ownership of Manchester United, the Red Devils could have...

1 ...cleared the estimated losses of the five biggest box office flops in cinematic history – *47 Ronin*, *Mars Needs Moms*, *The 13th Warrior*, *The Lone Ranger* and *RIPD* – at a total cost of £643.6 million, leaving them with enough small change to have fully financed big Oscar winner *Birdman*... three times over.

2 ...added a touch of class to the prawn sandwich brigade's matchday experience at the Theatre of Dreams by buying the four most expensive paintings sold at auction (adjusted for inflation): Gauguin's *When Will You Marry Me?*, Cezanne's *The Card Players*, Jackson Pollock's *No. 5, 1948* and Willem de Kooning's *Woman III*. And there should be a spare £80 million or so to spend on post-impressionist and abstract expressionist seafood butties.

3 ...rewarded the loyalty of United's 55,000 season ticket holders with a £9,295 Chevrolet Spark each as a 2015–16 renewal bonus. United would still have £168.7 million left over and shirt sponsor Chevvy would get free advertising, too!

£680,000,000

4 ...covered the cost of Arsenal's £390 million Emirates Stadium and the construction, football conversion and fit-out of Manchester City's Etihad Stadium, if they were feeling generous. Charity begins at home, after all.

5 ...bought the following XI (based on most recent transfer fees): Manuel Neuer, Dani Alves, David Luiz, Thiago Silva, Jordi Alba, Gareth Bale, Kaká, James Rodríguez, Mesut Özil, Zlatan Ibrahimović and Luis Suárez (oh, and substitutes: Thibaut Courtois, Nemanja Matić, Fernando Torres and Edinson Cavani).

6 ...purchased 66 and a half live Premier League matches under the latest TV rights deal and shown them exclusively on MUTV. They'd even be able to bring Gary Neville back as a pundit.

TOTAL £669.5M

"A LEVERAGED WHAT NOW?"

United fan, economist and former Goldman Sachs boss Jim O'Neill, who quit the club board when the Glazers took the club private in 2005, explains how the takeover was completed

WHAT IS A LEVERAGED BUYOUT?
A leveraged buyout is when you put up just a fraction of the cash that a business is being sold for and borrow the rest. Should it be allowed? As a general business procedure, yes. There's reasonable evidence that leveraged-buyout owners are good at extracting value. The Glazers did it to the book. Leveraged-buyout owners tend to own a company for seven years; they extract money, increase cash flow and cut or keep costs low. They then aim to float the business at a profit, with the debt repaid using money from a stock market launch.

SO WHAT'S THE PROBLEM?
If you look at the rise of the Premier League, United could have been as good as Barça in the last decade. Since the takeover, United have been marginally less successful. They stopped being in the market for top, game-changing players. It was only in the summer of 2014 that the club started spending again. Domestically, United could easily have competed with Chelsea's spending, but the club's strong incomes were used for repaying debt or the owners' personal income. The numbers that have been spent to repay the debt are vast.

AND WHAT HAPPENS NEXT?
In 2012, the Glazers raised money through a limited public offering on the New York Stock Exchange, which surprised me because other stock exchanges turned them down [flotations in Singapore and Hong Kong were called off due to lack of demand]. The way they did it means it will be difficult for others to try to buy the club. They paid £790m for United and put up only £250 million of their own funds. With the current share price it's worth £4.2 billion. The Glazers have been very clever. They've done it all ruthlessly well.

THE TAKEOVER
WHAT THE PLAYERS MADE OF IT ALL

"We didn't want to speak out" – a former player
offers his perspective on condition of anonymity

"I looked around Wembley during the 2010 League Cup Final and saw the United end with our fans – 30,000 to 40,000 of them. Green-and-gold scarves were everywhere; it looked like Aston Villa against Norwich. For the first time since the Glazer family takeover, I thought to myself, 'Our fans are really not happy here.' The players spoke about it privately, but never publicly. That would never have been approved.

The green-and-gold scarves appeared at the start of 2010. I first started seeing them when fans asked us for autographs. I thought, 'Why is a Norwich fan asking me for an autograph?' I knew fans were wearing them in the stadium, but they didn't stand out at first.

Over the months the numbers grew. David Beckham was pictured with one around his neck after United played AC Milan. Some fans saw him as a protestor, but I think a scarf was thrown to him and he put it around his neck.

He was a Milan player and didn't realise they were a form of protest.

I respected the fans' right to protest but it was hard for any of the players to speak out during the takeover. We weren't encouraged to and most weren't really that interested, or didn't understand what was going on. The squad was assured that everything was going to be fine and that was the end of it.

We realised that a lot of fans were against it but people are reluctant to speak out against their bosses. The players concentrated on football, not finances. Some had come from countries where football is run really badly.

They thought United was the best-run club they'd ever been at – and they were probably right. The manager assured us that everything was going to be all right and that was enough for the players.

He said that he and David Gill would remain at the club and that their roles wouldn't change. Both were trusted and respected by the players. Gill was a strong character – the only person I saw stand up to Ferguson and tell him he was wrong. I think even the manager appreciated that sometimes.

We could see the manager was getting some criticism at the time of the takeover, both from the media and even our own fans. So did David Gill, who had people turning up to his house. Both of them wanted the club to carry on as normal, and that's exactly what happened.

From a player's perspective, there were very few changes after the takeover because I think Sir Alex took it upon himself to protect both his staff and the players. The only change for us players was the extra commercial work after training. It went from a couple of players doing something once or twice a week to something happening every day.

There was a diary for all of that and loads of footballs to sign – they were lined up along a corridor. But signing footballs, many of which were going to charity, is hardly a chore, is it?

I don't think every player loved the commercial work, but what could they say? They were all being paid very well and a lot of the money coming in was from the club's commercial success, which the Glazers were driving forward.

WHAT'S THE WORST THAT COULD HAPPEN?

The Glazers aren't the only owners to share a 'complex' relationship with their club's fans

THE MADNESS OF KING GEORGE

Ex-safecracker George Reynolds was welcomed by fans of basement boys Darlington in 1999. He promised Premier League football and built a new stadium before promptly threatening and banning anybody who dared to criticise him. Reynolds became unpopular with Quakers fans as the team stagnated, stepping aside after the club went into administration in 2003. He was banged up for tax evasion two years later. Darlo dropped out of the Football League in 2010 and went bust in 2012.

THE EXPLOSIVE DON OF ZAGREB

"I'm going to stick YouTube on my d**k," said Zdravko Mamić in 2007. It was the irascible Dinamo Zagreb chief's response to clips of fans calling for his head. In 2011 Dithe Bad Blue Boys, Dinamo's ultras, stormed a press conference to confront the former businessman and agent about his mismanagement of the club (despite the team winning nine league titles in a row during his tenure). Assault, embezzlement, match-fixing: you name it, Mamić has at some point been accused of it.

JESUS COMMITS A CARDINAL SIN

Jesus Gil, the long-serving former owner of Atlético Madrid, wasn't all bad. The sight of the rotund former mayor of Marbella riding around Madrid on the back of an elephant to celebrate Atléti's 1996 Double triumph certainly registers in the 'plus' column. But Gil – now deceased – committed one act for which fans can never forgive him: in 1992 he shut down the club's youth team because there was "no point" in it, forcing young Atléti fan Raúl to defect to rivals Real Madrid. Oh well.

"GLAZERS OUT!"

In photo form, a decade of protest

MANC'S BUT NO YANK'S!

GLAZER - FOREVER IN YOUR DEBT

NOT FOR SALE

2BN STOLEN #GLAZERSOUT

ALDO CHARMS LEFTY LIVORNO

How not to endear yourself to Livorno fans, by club president Aldo Spinelli: 1) Threaten to "sell up and f**k off" every year, then don't; 2) Time and again call the Tuscan port a "Commie town"; 3) Call the club's stadium a "420-year-old lousy cesspit". Spinelli and his offensive charm have at least seen the Tuscan outfit compete in Europe for the first time ever in 2006. Honorable Serie A mentions go to Palermo's trigger-happy Maurizio Zamparini and, of course, Silvio 'Bunga' Berlusconi.

SWISSED OFF BY CHECHEN CHIEF

During a chaotic eight months from May 2011 to January 2012, mysterious Chechen benefactor Bulat Chagaev took Roy Hodgson's former club Neuchatel Xamax from the Swiss Premier League to bankruptcy and demotion to the fifth tier. As well as sacking several managers, Chagaev also axed Xamax's entire administrative staff, leaving the club unable to even print tickets. He also cut ties with the club's two biggest supporters' groups. It's fair to assume that they hate him, then.

RACING DOUBLE THEIR TROUBLE

Racing Santander take the biscuit for having had not one but two hated owners of late. In 2003, Ukrainian-American nutbar Dmitry Piterman made himself manager, which wasn't actually allowed. He then bought Alaves, who were soon relegated, and USL side California Victory, who folded after a season. Back in Santander, former owner Angel Lavin was attacked by fans in the directors' box in 2014 after two relegations in a row and continuing financial turmoil.

Words: Louis Massarella

FC UNITED
THE FANS TAKE BACK THEIR CLUB

A team that started out as an act of defiant protest has now become a success story in its own right

FC United of Manchester's 10th anniversary looks set to be a happy one, for a couple of very important reasons.

Firstly, their new 5,000-capacity ground, featuring a 26-step covered terrace that once stood at Northwich Victoria's Drill Field, should finally be open in time for a friendly match against a Benfica XI on 29 May.

Secondly, after seven years in the Evo-Stik League, FC United hope to play Manchester United's opponents in the 1968 European Cup Final as league champions, after winning promotion to Conference North. Their rise has come under the guidance of Karl Marginson, the former Rotherham, Macclesfield and Stalybridge Celtic midfielder who has managed FC United since the club's inception. He has now overseen four promotions.

Their fully covered Broadhurst Park home in Moston, a working-class area in north Manchester, cost £6.3 million, with £3 million raised by supporters (£2 million in community shares and £1 million cash and loan stock) from their 2,000-average home crowds.

They haven't got this far without the odd setback, though. Even completing their new home has been troublesome, with delays caused by one of the builders going bust – just one of many obstacles the club has faced.

General manager Andy Walsh has been there from the start. The idea of a breakaway club was raised in the now-defunct *Red Issue* fanzine, gaining momentum as fans realised the Glazer takeover was going to happen.

"I attended meetings about FC held by a steering committee, and while I couldn't believe the progress they'd made, I remained sceptical," explains Walsh. "Having defeated a planned Murdoch takeover in 1998, I thought we could do the same with the Glazers. I'd already renewed my season tickets for the 2005-06 season."

Walsh had been in contact with Alex Ferguson with the aim of getting the Scot to speak out against the buyout in a bid to spook the Glazers'

banks, but he failed to persuade the United manager to not back the takeover.

"Without his support, I think the takeover bid would have failed," said Walsh, but by 13 May 2005 the takeover became a formality as the Glazers acquired the necessary shares.

Ferguson was subsequently dismissive of FC United and their efforts as they climbed the

leagues from level 10 to level seven, where they missed out on promotion several times in the play-offs. Protests continued throughout that summer, with Walsh attending and chairing several meetings of fans. He'd been active in United-fan politics for a decade and was well respected. He cancelled his season tickets, which he'd already paid for.

"I stood outside the ticket office for 20 minutes and contemplated," he explains. "In the end it was my family who wanted to be part of FC United." Although he lives close to Old Trafford, in Stretford, he hasn't been to a single United game since.

The formation of FC United was met with a mixed reaction from Manchester United's hardcore match-going fans. Some were – and remain to this day – against the club, dubbing their fans 'Judases' for deserting the team they once supported. These same Red Devils supporters don't respect what they consider to be a 'preachy', 'supercilious'

"SOME MANCHESTER UNITED DIEHARDS ARE AGAINST FC UNITED, SEEING THEIR FANS AS 'PREACHY' AND SUPERCILIOUS"

attitude and are quick to rubbish claims that United's fan culture has been ruined.

Extreme views continue to exist on both sides, but the majority of United fans wish their non-league counterparts well and respect their achievements, even if they remain Manchester United supporters themselves.

"I'm still a Manchester United fan," counters Walsh. "I just don't support the Glazer business model. So we decided to do something new." Walsh is popular among FC United fans and respected by many within football, but he has had a hard ride at times.

"I've had threats," he admits. "I've had people who have come up to me in the street in Manchester and been very aggressive, but after a little talk we've either agreed to disagree or they've seen what we're doing."

FC United's members have voted collectively against shirt sponsorship, stadium naming

rights and even showing Sky television in the clubhouse of their new home.

"As football fans, we were always told: 'take it or leave it'," Walsh explains. "We're showing there is an alternative way of doing things – an enjoyable way that makes football accessible to all."

The Glazers' leveraged buyout was a tipping point for many FC United fans, but it wasn't the only issue. Ticket prices were a big gripe for the newer club's followers (who now pay just £8 for home games), as were the changing demographics at Old Trafford and television's grip on kick-off times. However, though largely successful, FC United's first decade did hit some rough spots.

"There was a time when I thought the club wouldn't pull through, after a site for our ground in Newton Heath was pulled," admits Walsh. "But we've come through every setback stronger." With opposition to a new football ground from a minority of neighbours, the recession cutting deep

and local authorities making cutbacks, FC United had significant assistance from a Manchester City Council enthused by the idea of a community-minded football club.

They also got a £500,000 grant from the Football Foundation, a third of which comes from the Premier League football that so many FC United fans have turned their backs on.

Asked whether the priority is for FC United to rise up the leagues or focus on community work, Walsh says both. "We're a football club first – if we're not, then everything else fails. But a club should be part of the community."

Adjacent to FC United's home is a 3G pitch, which provides training facilities for the club's other sides, including a strong women's team, and it also gives local sides such as Moston Juniors somewhere to play.

With that in mind, leaving politics aside, you can see how and why FC United is a valuable venture.

FERGIE'S

DOUBLE

MOSCOW 2008

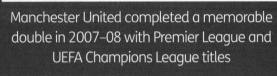

Manchester United completed a memorable double in 2007–08 with Premier League and UEFA Champions League titles

Words Michael E Haskew

After three seasons in the doldrums, Manchester United bounced back with a resurgent campaign in 2006–07, winning the Premier League title by six points over rivals Chelsea, finishing runners-up in the FA Cup final, and reaching the semi-finals of the UEFA Champions League.

Such a performance offered promise for the future, but there remained work to be done, and Sir Alex Ferguson knew it. For the 2007–08 season, he sought depth to augment his powerful line-up. The United mastermind made moves to shore up the core of standout performers that had propelled the team to relevance once again. Carlos Tevez arrived from West Ham on loan for two years, while Owen Hargreaves was signed from Bayern Munich, Anderson from Porto, and Nani from Sporting Lisbon. The last two of these required a combined investment of over £31m, but the dividend would come in due time.

Tevez joined the most potent attack in the Premier League and perhaps the world with superstar Cristiano Ronaldo and stalwart performer Wayne Rooney, while the midfield boasted experience in the likes of Ryan Giggs and Paul Scholes, ably assisted by Michael Carrick. The back four of Wes Brown, Patrice Evra, Rio Ferdinand and Nemanja Vidić were among the best of the era, while veteran Dutch goalkeeper Edwin van der Sar and Polish deputy Tomasz Kuszczak were a solid last line of defence.

Following a mixed set of preseason results, the Red Devils kicked off 2007–08 with a penalty shootout victory over rivals Chelsea in the FA Community Shield. Then, with the opening of the Premier League

WINNERS

season, a rumble of discontent emerged from the United faithful amid a disappointing early run. Starting with draws against Reading and Portsmouth and a derby defeat at Manchester City, the team lost Ronaldo to suspension for a headbutt in the Portsmouth match and Rooney to a foot injury against Reading. Finding themselves 17th in the table, United finally picked up their first win of the season on 26 August against Tottenham Hotspur at Old Trafford.

A string of seven more victories followed. While they conceded just four goals in their first 11 matches, scoring was slow until Ronaldo, Rooney and Tevez finally clicked in October, netting nine of 12 goals in a three-match run. Although a ten-game unbeaten run came to an end on 24 November at the Reebok Stadium in a 1-0 loss to Bolton Wanderers, five straight wins followed in December before a 1-0 loss to West Ham in the last league game of 2007.

In the Champions League, meanwhile, United emerged from the group stage with 16 points from six games. The Red Devils ensured their passage to the knockout stage with a 4-0 win against Dynamo Kyiv at Old Trafford in their fourth group match as Tevez, Rooney, Ronaldo and Gerard Piqué scored. A win against Sporting Lisbon in the next game secured top spot and allowed Ferguson to take a youthful squad to Italy for the final game against Roma on 7 December, which ended 1-1.

Tevez scored the only goal as the Reds defeated Birmingham City in the first Premier League match of the new year, and Ronaldo got a hat-trick in a 6-0 rout of Newcastle. Shaking off the frustrations of the early season, Ronaldo gained momentum, putting together a string of dazzling performances in the early spring, maturing before the eyes of the football world from an adept wideman to perhaps the most complete player the Premier League had ever witnessed.

On 21 December the draw for the first knockout round of the Champions League paired United with Lyon. The first leg in France on 20 February 2008 ended in a 1-1 draw as Tevez netted in the 87th minute. Two weeks later, the Red Devils won the home leg 1-0, Ronaldo scoring from a

narrow angle to help United reach the quarter-finals.

On 8 March, United were knocked out of the FA Cup, losing 1-0 to Portsmouth in the quarter-finals after Tomasz Kuszczak, who had replaced the injured van der Sar at half-time, was sent off. From the resulting penalty, Sulley Muntari scored against stand-in keeper Rio Ferdinand. Still, at the end of the month they held a six-point lead over Arsenal in the league following a 4-0 rout of Aston Villa on the 29th at Old Trafford. Ronaldo back-heeled a ball through an opponent's legs only 16 minutes in, then assisted Tevez, who headed home his teammate's cross. Rooney stepped up with a brace, finishing a pair of assists from Ronaldo and narrowly missing out on a hat-trick after an offside call.

As Arsenal and Chelsea struggled to remain in Premier League contention, the Red Devils battled stubborn opposition and injuries. Van der Sar's timely block salvaged a draw at Middlesbrough, while Ronaldo scored a penalty and Owen Hargreaves

Clockwise from above Scholes celebrates his winner against Barcelona; Ronaldo and Rooney formed a devastating partnership; Roma fans express their displeasure; Hargreaves curls home a crucial free kick against Arsenal; Giggs clinches the title with United's second goal at Wigan; Fergie parades his tenth Premier League title; Ronaldo clutches the Champions League trophy following victory over Chelsea; Carlos Tevez and Chelsea skipper John Terry exchange a few words during the final in Moscow

lofted a free kick over the wall and into the bottom-left corner of the net for a crucial 2-1 triumph over visiting Arsenal. The win put United six points ahead of Chelsea and nine in front of Arsenal.

However, a draw against Blackburn Rovers at Ewood Park made things tight going into the final stretch. By the end of April, a victory over Chelsea would have given the Red Devils the edge and left them needing only a single point to secure the Premier League crown. However, Chelsea would not go down without a fight. A 2-1 loss at Stamford Bridge left the two teams level on points, however, United's superior goal difference meant that wins in their last two matches would all but guarantee them the title. Ronaldo netted a pair while Tevez and Michael Carrick contributed to a comfortable 4-1 win over visiting West Ham United on 3 May, setting the stage for the final act at Wigan on 11 May. Going into the game, United knew that they simply had to equal or better the Chelsea result at Bolton to take the Premier League title.

Initially it seemed that Wigan hadn't read the script, the hosts repelling every United attack and Paul Scholes receiving a booking for a rash tackle. Moments later, a Wigan

"THE IRREPRESSIBLE GIGGS CONFIDENTLY SLOTTED IN HIS SUDDEN-DEATH KICK"

shot appeared to hit the outstretched arm of Rio Ferdinand but the referee waved away calls for a penalty. Just after the half-hour mark, United were awarded a penalty of their own, which Ronaldo deftly converted. In the second half, Wigan keeper Chris Kirkland kept United at bay.

As rain began to fall, Sir Alex looked to shore things up, as well as nick a decisive second goal. He introduced Hargreaves to the action, and Ryan Giggs, club captain standing in for the injured Gary Neville, came on in the 68th minute to equal Sir Bobby Charlton's remarkable record of 758 club appearances.

"As soon as the rain came," Ferguson recalled, "I knew I should get Giggsy on because he loves the soft ground."

Wigan were tenacious, but Giggs delivered, slipping the ball past Kirkland after a slide-rule pass from Rooney. Chelsea's draw with Bolton meant that Manchester United secured their 17th Premier League title without the need for goal difference. It was a close-run thing.

"We had some nervous moments and then the rain came and anything could have happened," said Ferguson afterwards. "We started to get a grip of it after half-time, though. I was thinking, 'Please give me the second goal.'"

Over the course of the Premier League season United won 27 games, lost five, and drew six. Their lightning attack scored 80 goals, with Ronaldo netting 31 in his fifth season with the Red Devils. The trio of Ronaldo, Tevez and Rooney combined for 57 goals, while the defence proved watertight, conceding only 22 goals and finishing with 21 clean sheets. While van der Sar led the way in goal, Scholes and Carrick were masterful in midfield. Ferguson was also at his mercurial best, utilising a hybrid 4-4-2/4-3-3 system that played to his team's strengths and kept opponents off balance at critical moments.

Yet United were not just fighting for glory on one front. As they blitzed their way to domestic victory in the league they also faced a string of tests in Europe that would ultimately define their season.

On 1 April, United had returned to the Italian capital for the first leg of the quarter-finals. Goals from Ronaldo and Rooney gave them a 2-0 advantage, and the Reds progressed to the next round eight days later as Tevez scored in the 70th minute.

In the semi-finals they came up against Spanish giants Barcelona. A cagey first leg at the Camp Nou finished 0-0 after Ronaldo missed a penalty, however, roared on by a boisterous home crowd in the second leg, Scholes scored the decisive goal in the 14th minute to give United their 12th consecutive Champions League home win and set up the first all-English final in the competition's history against rivals Chelsea.

The epic Champions League final, played at Luzhniki Stadium in Moscow on 21 May 2008, remains a classic. United started on the front foot, with Ronaldo opening the scoring in the 26th minute with a header from a Wes Brown cross, his 42nd goal of a remarkable season that led to the first of his five Ballon d'Or awards. Just before half-time, van der Sar slipped and Frank Lampard scored for Chelsea to even the match. As each team saw opportunities come and go – Chelsea twice hitting the woodwork – Didier Drogba was sent off for slapping Vidić. The advantage came to nothing, however, with the game heading for extra time and then penalties as the rain steadily fell.

With two penalties scored a piece, Ronaldo saw his kick turned away by Blues keeper Petr Čech. With the chance to win it, Chelsea captain John Terry

stepped up, but as he went to strike the ball his standing foot slipped and his penalty crashed against the post.

The irrepressible Giggs, breaking Bobby Charlton's appearance record, confidently slotted in his sudden-death kick, before van der Sar easily turned aside Nicolas Anelka's decisive penalty. Cue wild celebrations.

Manchester United, in a stellar campaign, had captured their third European Cup and secured a historic double. Ronaldo observed, "In my opinion, I played well in the game, scored a goal, and then missed the penalty. It would have been the worst day of my life. We deserved to win as we played better in the whole game. It means everything to me. We have won both trophies. It is the best day in my life."

It was also arguably a triumph for Ferguson that stood alongside the historic treble of 1999, given the financial might and formidable pedigree of the Chelsea side his charges had seen off on two fronts. To this day United remain the only side to win the Champions League and the Premier League in the same season – a season that no United fan will ever forget.

Images Alamy (Busby Babes), Getty Images, Liewig Christian/Corbis/Getty Images (Rooney/Ronaldo, Roma), Getty Images/John Peters/Manchester United (group training), Henri Szwarc/Icon Sport/Getty Images (Tevez/Terry)

> ## "I WAS F**KING HAPPY EDWIN SAVED ANELKA'S PENALTY.
> # I WAS NEXT... AND WOULDN'T HAVE SCORED"

In 2008, Rio Ferdinand added his name to an exclusive list of Manchester United captains to lift Ol' Big Ears – and changed his life forever. He recalls the ecstasy of victory in Moscow, plus more defining moments that made him playing for West Ham, Leeds and England

Words Chris Flanagan **Portraits** Robert Wilson

The time was 1.45 a.m. when Bobby Charlton approached Rio Ferdinand. Almost 12 years on, as he sits in front of *FFT*, there's still a slight tremble in Ferdinand's voice as he recalls the words that followed.

The duo were stood inside Moscow's Luzhniki Stadium, and Ferdinand was moments away from collecting the Champions League trophy as Manchester United captain. Minutes earlier, long past midnight in the Russian capital, United had beaten Chelsea on penalties – 40 years after the club's maiden European Cup triumph and 50 on from the Munich air disaster.

"As Chelsea were going to get their medals, Sir Bobby came to the bottom of the steps," Ferdinand tells *FFT* now. "He said, 'Rio, do you know what this means?' Even though we'd just won the Champions League final, I hadn't given it any thought. He said, 'Rio, you're the third person to lift this trophy for this club, and I'm one of them as well. This will change your life.' He's a legend for club and country. He said some other words too, and they were just beautiful. I started getting all emotional."

In that moment, Ferdinand had reached the pinnacle of a glorious career; one in which he twice became the most expensive defender in the world, won six Premier League titles and amassed 81 caps for England. Among centre-backs, only Bobby Moore and Billy Wright have ever earned more.

• • •

Such greatness never seemed possible for Ferdinand as a youngster growing up in Peckham, south London. Back then, he had another hobby – aged 11, he received a scholarship to attend the Central School of Ballet. If it seemed an unlikely choice, ultimately it would help his ambitions of becoming a footballer. "Strength, suppleness, poise, balance – it enhanced all of those things," he says.

Ferdinand's graceful skills were initially deployed in midfield. He was later asked to move into defence but wasn't keen on the idea. "I was 14 and someone said, 'Rio, I don't want you to play in central midfield any more, I want you to play centre-back'," he remembers. "Being a centre-back wasn't fashionable – I wanted to be a central midfielder who scored goals and was the star.

"They said, 'Yeah, but I think you've got a better chance of being a defender.' I think I sulked for about two or three weeks, but then I realised, 'Actually, you know what? This is my best route if I want to be a professional footballer.'"

Indeed it was. Ferdinand would swiftly make a career for himself as a ball-playing centre half. "I was still doing midfielder things as a defender, which probably helped me stand out from other kids," he says. "My brother showed me a video the other day. He'd pulled an old VHS out of his loft – it was a youth team game for West Ham against Wimbledon at Upton Park, against Carl Cort. I went to clear the ball down the line, then chopped back, did a bit of skill and ran forward. As a centre-back, I was doing things that midfielders would normally do. It was a feather in my cap."

Ferdinand joined West Ham United after interest from numerous London clubs including Charlton Athletic, Chelsea, Millwall and QPR, and even Middlesbrough in the North East. "I bought into what West Ham were saying," he explains. "They had an idea about how they wanted their club to run. They were investing money and time into youth team players, getting them into the first team. When I heard that, I thought, 'I've got a chance here, I'm going to sign.'

"They were true to their word and it wasn't just me – it was Frank Lampard, Michael Carrick, Joe Cole, Glen Johnson, Jermain Defoe, my brother Anton and loads more who went on to play in the lower leagues. From my era, there must have been 20-25 in those two or three age groups who played professionally."

When Ferdinand was 17, Harry Redknapp handed him a first-team debut against Sheffield Wednesday in May 1996. "Harry enabled me to go out there and make mistakes without feeling the

pressure," says Ferdinand. "He'd say, 'Rio, go and do your thing – play out from the back and run out a bit. It makes you look brilliant, but don't keep making the same mistake.'

"That's a vital bit of information from a coach or manager for any youngster – it gives you the confidence to go out there and express yourself. Don't be scared to make mistakes, but keep learning while you're doing it and don't make the same errors time and time again. I made a lot when I was a kid in the first team, which led to goals or chances against us. But I knew that the manager believed in me, so I carried on playing."

Ferdinand developed into one of the world's brightest talents over 158 appearances for the Hammers under Redknapp. He'd only just turned 22 when Leeds United paid £18 million for him in November 2000, making him the most expensive defender of all time. With the price tag came a certain amount of pressure.

"The most pressure I felt was when I went to have the fitness test before you sign, and all the youth team were watching," he smiles now. "I had to pass the ball to the physio, and the physio would just keep passing it back. I was probably never so nervous in

"THE BE ALL AND END ALL FOR ME WAS TO WIN TROPHIES, AND MANCHESTER UNITED WOULD GIVE ME A GREAT CHANCE. I DIDN'T WANT TO END MY CAREER WITH NOTHING"

Left and below Making his name at West Ham; before returning as an £18m man with Leeds
Above right "Oi, get out of my pocket, Batigol…"

my whole career, because all the young kids were watching me and thinking, 'What does £18m buy you?' That was pressure, man.

"But my mates never spoke to me about money – that wasn't my motivation. My motivation was playing football at the highest level I could. A boy from my estate, signing for Leeds and getting to play Champions League football."

In his first season at Elland Road, Ferdinand reached a Champions League semi-final, scoring his opening goal for the club in a 3-0 win over Deportivo La Coruña in the last eight. "That season was crazy," he says. "Leeds were on a great run – when I joined, they'd beaten Milan and knocked out Barcelona. I thought we were going to win it that year, but we played a great Valencia team in the semi-finals. They smashed us up 3-0 in Spain."

Perhaps it was a sign of Ferdinand's ambition that even a run to the Champions League semi-finals didn't give him the feeling that he'd made it as a player at the top level. "Not really, because we'd gone out," he insists. "I still felt like I had lots to do. I thought, 'Wow, that Valencia team are a few strings ahead of us' – and they didn't even win the final against Bayern Munich. Although I was playing well, I wasn't where I wanted to be yet."

After another impressive season for Leeds, though, he was ready to start for England at the 2002 World Cup. They were his first-ever appearances at a major tournament – Ferdinand was part of Glenn Hoddle's France 98 squad without seeing any action, and narrowly missed out on selection for Euro 2000 under Kevin Keegan.

After helping Sven-Goran Eriksson's side beat Argentina 1-0 in the group stage, he scored with a header against Denmark in the last 16 – even if it needed an assist from goalkeeper Thomas Sorensen, who inadvertently bundled the ball over the line. "I made sure I got that goal because it could have been taken off me – it wasn't actually on target!" smiles the 41 year old.

"But that tournament was the time when I started thinking, 'I'm a top player and I'll go on to be a top player.' I played and just felt comfortable in that setting, under that pressure. We were up against a good Argentina team and there was a lot riding on it. I had to deal with someone like Gabriel Batistuta. He was their main goal threat – he was the man back then." Ferdinand jokingly looks downwards to inspect his pocket. "He could still be in there somewhere!"

• • •

Ferdinand wasn't the only one who thought he would become a top player after the World Cup – Alex Ferguson did too, sealing a £29.3m deal for the 23 year old within a month of Brazil lifting the trophy. Leeds had missed out on Champions League qualification, so when the defender learned of Manchester United's interest, he refused to leave chairman Peter Ridsdale's office for six hours, insisting a move be agreed to take him to Old Trafford.

"There was no way I wasn't going," he reveals. "I would have done anything. The be all and end all for me as a kid was to win trophies. I got to the point where I was seeing others with loads, and I didn't want to end my career without anything in my cabinet. I knew that joining United would give me a great chance."

"WHEN JOHN TERRY STEPPED UP I THOUGHT IT WAS ALL OVER. I'D WATCHED HIM TAKE PENALTIES IN TRAINING, AND HE'D ALWAYS BEEN SO COOL AND CALM UNDER PRESSURE"

The transfer made him the world's most expensive defender for a second time, after French World Cup winner Lilian Thuram pipped him with a £23m switch to Juventus in 2001.

FFT asks what Ferdinand remembers most about that day. "Other than the suit?" he laughs, recalling the garish white outfit he donned for his unveiling. "It was an unbelievable day – although when I signed, I remember Alex Ferguson asking my mum, 'Is he all right, he doesn't seem happy?' She said, 'Until he starts playing, you won't see the enjoyment – you'll see it when he plays.'

"The thing I remember most is the press conference, because they asked, 'What do you want to get out of this move?' I said that when I finally left Man United, if I could walk out of Old Trafford with my head held high, having etched my name somewhere in the history of the club, that would mean I'd done well – that meant trophies." He achieved exactly that. "Yeah," he smiles. "They were the best years of my playing career. It was hard work over a long period of time, with a great bunch of people."

Among those people was his long-time central defensive partner Nemanja Vidić. "We just gelled," says Ferdinand. "In a partnership, having the same attributes makes it more difficult to work as a pair. We had some similarities, but there were also some big differences between us. I liked sweeping up behind – if there was any problem for anyone, I liked to be the security blanket. Vida loved to attack the ball first. He was the aggressor."

They were also united by a motivation to win Ferguson's approval. "He was different to Harry Redknapp in that he didn't really praise me – he was fearful that maybe I'd get big-headed and think I was the man," explains Ferdinand. "He thought that a lot about people from London – I think he had a certain idea about how Londoners are. But it was probably good for me that he didn't, as I always felt that I had something to prove to him. Me and Vida were the same like that – we used to talk about it a lot.

"Sir Alex would say, 'Cristiano, Rooney, Tevez, Berbatov, Giggs and Scholes – brilliant', but he'd never really name-check us. We used to think, 'We're keeping clean sheets every other week here – what's going on?!' But it kept us hungry. We wanted to prove ourselves to him and get the recognition that we both felt we deserved. It was a great bit of management."

Naturally, there was a hairdryer or two as well. "The main one was after a game at Bayern Munich [in March 2010]," recalls Ferdinand. "I disagreed with his tactics in that game. We lost 2-1 and I thought we should have done something different, so I was screaming and shouting. Then he walked in and just shut the place down with his screaming and shouting over mine!"

Looking back, who was right that night? "I was right, because we lost!" he smiles. "But I think he appreciated that when I'd shout or resist against certain things, tactics or something he was saying, it wasn't from a selfish point of view. It was from a team perspective, because I wanted us to do well."

• • •

Ferdinand would go to another World Cup with England in 2006 and impress again: Eriksson's men conceded only twice in five matches. "I saw a stat the other day: I played ten matches at the World Cup and kept seven clean sheets – that's an unbelievable stat, so all the strikers just never did their jobs!" he says. "I loved the big occasions and the big matches – the build-up, everything about them. I loved playing for England at World Cups."

That Ferdinand excelled there said plenty about him, considering many regard the World Cup as the ultimate test of a player's ability. "I don't agree – the Champions League is," he insists. "You go to the World Cup and no disrespect, but you can be playing Peru or some country that's ranked 200th in the world. The Champions League is the elite of the elite – by a smidgen, I think that's the most difficult competition to win."

When asked to pick his best-ever performance, it's perhaps little wonder that he chooses a game from the 2007–08 campaign, and United's run to Champions League glory. "The Camp Nou," he says, referencing the night when United returned home with a 0-0 draw from the first leg of their semi-final, going on to win the second 1-0. "We kept a clean sheet in both legs of that semi against Barcelona, with their forward line: Samuel Eto'o, Lionel Messi and Thierry Henry.

"They had some ridiculous players, and over 180 minutes we kept them out. Not just for me as an individual, but as a team, it was our best defensive performance. That was all about concentration – it's one of the biggest assets for any defender."

Then came that final against Chelsea in Moscow. "It was a crazy night, something that will live long in my memory," he says. "It was a mountain you thought you'd never be able to get up and conquer."

When John Terry stepped up to take Chelsea's fifth penalty in the shootout, did Ferdinand think United's hopes of victory were over? "Yeah," he admits. "I'd watched him take penalties in training with England, and he'd always been so cool and calm under pressure. At that point, I didn't see it turning out the way it did."

Terry slipped on the sodden surface and hit the woodwork, taking the shootout to sudden death. Anderson and Ryan Giggs converted United's sixth and seventh penalties before Edwin van der Sar kept out Nicolas Anelka's spot-kick to secure victory.

"I was next, so I was f**king happy Edwin saved Anelka's penalty," says Ferdinand, revealing that he was eighth on the Red Devils' list. "My legs were jelly and I didn't know what was going to happen – I wouldn't have scored, man. I was too nervous.

"When we finally won, the feeling was unbelievable. The only way I've described it is if you could bottle that emotion and sell it, you'd become a billionaire. You don't get that feeling anywhere else. To be a football player and conquer that... it's f**king mad."

That ability to challenge for the biggest honours with United was what persuaded him to turn down offers from the most high-profile overseas clubs. "Fabio Capello tried to take me to Roma when I was at West Ham, and later on I received offers from both Real Madrid and Barcelona," he admits. "But when you get to Manchester United and you're winning, it's hard to leave that. Winning is an addiction, and once I was at United, I felt I was at the top of the tree.

"The times when I got offers to go to Real Madrid and Barcelona, they were in transition. I'd have been leaving and hoping they came back to being great again in the next two or three years. But I didn't want to wait. I was winning then and wanted to continue winning."

Ferdinand won ten major trophies during his Manchester United career, even if they eluded him at international level with England. He never played at the European Championship, having been banned in 2004 for missing a drugs test. He was due to skipper the Three Lions at the 2010 World Cup, but injury struck a week before the start of the tournament. "That killed me," he sighs. "But sometimes you play your best games when you're not there, because we were terrible."

Ferdinand's legacy for club and country was already secure – he is rightly regarded as one of England's finest centre-backs. "It's nice when people say stuff like that," he smiles. "You play football to win trophies and earn respect from your peers. I always knew my worth in the team I was in. If I wasn't there, I wanted all the other players to think, 'We're not as good when Rio doesn't play.' I'd like to think I got somewhere near that."

Of that, there is little doubt. When a poll was conducted recently to select England's greatest team, Ferdinand was picked to partner Bobby Moore at centre-back. And as was pointed out to him shortly before 2 a.m. on that 2008 night in Moscow, only three players have ever lifted the European Cup for Manchester United: Bobby Charlton, Peter Schmeichel and Rio Ferdinand. It's not bad company to keep.

Anti-clockwise from far left "What on earth are you wearing, lad?!"; Ferdinand calls one of these two players "the aggressor..."; "Come on, Carra, we're never going to do the Hokey Cokey"; the night Rio conquered a mountain in Moscow

MORE ON FOURFOURTWO.COM

• Nemanja Vidić: You Ask The Questions *(by Andy Mitten)*

• When Alex Ferguson got sacked at St Mirren *(by Thore Haugstad)*

• Quiz: United's Champions League scorers of the last 10 seasons

PREMIER LEAGUE

UNITED'S FIGHT
TO RETURN TO THE TOP

Nine years ago, United bade farewell to Sir Alex Ferguson. Since then,
they've watched as five managers have struggled to replace him.
Yet there may now finally be genuine cause for optimism

Words Sam Pilger

Images Getty Images

Two days after winning United's third European Cup on a rain-soaked night in Moscow, Sir Alex Ferguson was back at the club's Carrington training ground to treat a group of journalists to a few glasses of celebratory champagne.

He confided in them that he would continue for only two more years. "Three at the very, very, very most," he said. "I'll definitely not be managing at 70. You have to think of time for yourself. And my wife is getting older."

Ferguson still had much he wanted to accomplish during this remaining time, including winning another Champions League to close the gap between United's three and Liverpool's five, and overtaking Liverpool's 18 league titles.

In the close season he broke United's transfer record to sign Dimitar Berbatov from Tottenham for £30.75 million and persuaded Cristiano Ronaldo to spurn the interest of Real Madrid to remain at Old Trafford.

The 2008–09 season began slowly, but once Ronaldo returned from injury in September to complete United's attack, Ferguson's side built momentum and went on a run of 16 unbeaten league games between November and March to reach the top of the table.

Despite a 4-1 defeat to main challengers Liverpool in March, United held firm, securing dramatic wins against Tottenham and Aston Villa to grasp a third consecutive title, making Ferguson the first manager to achieve this on two occasions.

In December 2008, United also became world champions for a second time, winning the FIFA Club World Cup final 1-0 against the Ecuadorian side LDU Quito in Yokohama, courtesy of a goal from Wayne Rooney. In March 2009 they added the League Cup, drawing 0-0 with Tottenham in normal time before triumphing in a penalty shoot-out in the final at Wembley.

In the Champions League, United overcame Inter Milan, Porto and Arsenal in the knockout rounds to set up a final against Barcelona in Rome. As the reigning European champions, United were favourites, but after dominating the first ten minutes they visibly shrank and had no answer to the joyous football played by the Catalan side, who won 2-0 courtesy of goals from Samuel Eto'o and Lionel Messi.

"It was just one-sided; they played the tiki-taka we now know all about, while we were wide open and just chasing shadows," Rio Ferdinand has since recalled.

The final was Ronaldo's last game before he joined Real Madrid for £80 million – then a world-record transfer fee – but Ferguson

surprisingly failed to reinvest most of this back into his squad, only adding the modest trio of Antonio Valencia from Wigan, an ageing Michael Owen and an unknown French winger in Gabriel Obertan.

Despite the loss of their Ballon d'Or winner and also Carlos Tevez to Manchester City, United came close to winning a fourth consecutive title, taking the race to the final weekend before finishing a point behind Chelsea.

They had more joy in the League Cup, beating Aston Villa 2-0 in the final with goals from Owen and Wayne Rooney, who filled Ronaldo's void during the 2009–10 season, scoring 34 goals and being voted the Footballer of the Year.

It was in September 2002 that Ferguson had declared, "My greatest challenge is not what's happening at the moment – my greatest challenge was knocking Liverpool right off their f***ing perch. And you can print that."

By the end of the 2010–11 season, he achieved his ambition by winning United's 19th title to overtake Liverpool. United remained unbeaten in their first 24 league games and didn't lose until the start of February to finish nine points ahead of Chelsea.

United were powered by Berbatov, Rooney, the Portuguese winger Nani and Mexican striker Javier Hernandez – known as 'Chicharito' – who had signed for just £6 million in the summer. This quartet scored 67 goals between them.

United also reached their third Champions League final in four seasons, where they faced Barcelona again. In the build-up, Ferguson had spoken about not being terrified of the "Barcelona carousel" – the quick passing of Xavi, Andrés Iniesta and Lionel Messi – but over 90 minutes they still had no solutions to it and slumped to a 3-1 defeat.

"Barcelona were easily the best team ever to line up against my United sides," Ferguson has said. "The Barcelona side that beat us at Wembley in 2011 was [also] superior to the one that conquered us in Rome two years earlier."

Below United celebrate winning the 2011 Premier League, their 19th overall title, to overtake Liverpool and become the most successful English side ever **Right** David De Gea and Louis van Gaal lift the FA Cup at Wembley after defeating Crystal Palace in the 2016 final

"[AFTER CITY SNATCHED THE TITLE] THE BOSS WALKED UP AND DOWN TELLING US, 'DON'T YOU EVER FORGET WHAT THIS FEELS LIKE'"

Since 2008 Manchester City had been transformed by the ownership of Sheikh Mansour, a billionaire member of the royal family of Abu Dhabi, who had spent millions assembling a new squad. Ferguson had dismissed City as "noisy neighbours", but by the 2011–12 season they were ready to turn up the volume.

United were given an early warning when City handed them a humiliating 6-1 defeat at Old Trafford, but by the spring they had an eight-point lead. Then United suffered a slip, losing to Wigan, drawing with Everton and losing 1-0 to City, to put their rivals top.

On the final day of the season, United needed to better City's result to win the title. They won their game 1-0 over Sunderland and learned City were losing 2-1 to QPR, with their game now in added time. But almost immediately City equalised, and just 125 seconds later news filtered through they had scored again through Sergio Agüero to snatch the title on goal difference. "We were champions for 30 seconds," Ferguson has recalled.

"The United players were devastated. Several of them were sitting slumped on the floor, silent, heads in their hands," former United defender Patrice Evra has said.

On the coach back to Manchester, however, Ferguson was already using the experience to inspire his squad. "The boss walked up and down the aisle, telling us, 'Don't you ever forget what this feels like'," Michael Carrick has said. "'Let this motivate you to win the league next year.'"

It had been speculated Ferguson was preparing to retire at the end of that season, but losing the title in such a cruel manner persuaded him to stay for another season with the aim of walking away as a champion.

To achieve that, Ferguson pulled off an incredible coup by signing the reigning Footballer of the Year, Robin van Persie, from Arsenal for £24 million.

The Dutchman became one of his best signings, scoring 26 league goals to help United regain the title, finishing 11 points ahead of

Above José Mourinho poses with the Europa League trophy after his United side had beaten Ajax in the 2017 final
Bottom A delighted Sir Alex Ferguson lifts his 13th and final Premier League title aloft

Manchester City. "He brought a Cantona-esque quality to an already very good side," said Ferguson.

The United manager had the happy ending he wanted to finish his incredible reign at Old Trafford and announced his retirement on 8 May 2013. "I'm going out a winner," he told his players when he informed them he was leaving. After 26 years, 1,500 games and 38 major trophies, Ferguson departed Old Trafford as the most successful manager in the history of English football.

One of his final acts at Old Trafford was to choose his successor, and he recommended the United board appoint the Everton manager David Moyes.

As a fellow hardened Glaswegian, Ferguson saw something of himself in Moyes and had been impressed with what he had achieved at Goodison Park. While he might not have won a trophy, he had finished in the top half of the table in nine of his 11 seasons.

Ferguson's expectation was once Moyes began working with better players and a bigger budget his managerial skills would see him flourish, but it didn't work out like that and almost immediately Moyes looked out of his depth.

He was not helped by the club's failure in that summer's transfer market; having been promised several marquee signings, including Gareth Bale, Cesc Fàbregas and even Ronaldo, he had to settle for just Marouane Fellaini from Everton.

Nonetheless, Moyes still had enough quality to challenge for trophies having inherited the reigning champions, but he suffered three defeats in his first six league games and never gained control over a fast-unravelling season. Moyes wore the look of a haunted man, who from September was locked outside the top four. By March it was consecutive 3-0 home defeats to Liverpool and Manchester City that provoked a 'Moyes Out' banner to be flown over Old Trafford. Following a 2-0 defeat to Everton in April Moyes was sacked, having taken United from first to seventh.

"Moyes never solved the football problems he faced," former Red Devils defender Rio Ferdinand has said. "He brought ideas and tactics, which worked for him at Everton, but didn't adapt to the expectations of United... He created a negative vibe where with Fergie it had always been positive."

United turned to Louis van Gaal, a manager with a wealth of experience who had enjoyed success at Ajax, Barcelona and Bayern Munich and who had just spent the summer of 2014 guiding the Netherlands to the World Cup semi-finals.

United immediately backed him in the transfer market, signing Ángel Di María, Luke Shaw, Ander Herrera, Daley Blind, Marcos Rojo, and Radamel Falcao (on loan) for a combined outlay of around £146 million.

Despite this influx of talent, after ten league games United were ninth. It was their worst start to a season since 1986–87, which had led to Ron Atkinson being sacked. Van Gaal did eventually manage to stabilise United's season with a run of only two defeats from their next 22 league games to climb to a fourth-placed finish.

Under Van Gaal there were complaints his football was too defensive, and some of his players did not enjoy his strict instructions and rigid structure, which allowed for little flair or creativity.

Crystal Palace in the final at Wembley, Jesse Lingard scoring a spectacular winner in extra-time. However, this was not enough to save the Dutchman, and two days after lifting the FA Cup United terminated his contract. Not everyone was happy about it. "I was devastated when Louis was sacked," the United captain Wayne Rooney has said. "For me, it was an absolute joy to work with him. We should have kept him for a third season."

Instead, United turned to José Mourinho, the revered former Porto, Chelsea, Inter Milan and Real Madrid manager, who had been sacked from his second spell with Chelsea the previous December and been waiting for United.

Once again United hoped an expensive foray into the transfer market would inspire a revival, and they brought in Zlatan Ibrahimović, Eric Bailly and Henrikh Mkhitaryan then broke the world transfer record to sign their former player Paul Pogba from Juventus for £89.1 million.

In the Premier League, Mourinho's United endured a frustrating season; they were difficult to beat, losing only five times – the same as the eventual champions Chelsea – but they drew too many games, which kept them rooted to sixth in the table for four months before eventually finishing there.

In the cup competitions this side was a different beast, and after winning the Community Shield against Leicester City in Mourinho's first game, United added the League Cup with a 3-2 victory over Southampton in the final in February, with two goals from Ibrahimović and one from Lingard.

Towards the end of the season, Mourinho began to prioritise the Europa League over the Premier League, believing it was United's best route back to the Champions League. They duly reached the final in Stockholm, where they would face Ajax.

United became only the fifth side to win all three major European trophies by defeating the Dutch side 2-0 with goals from Pogba and Mkhitaryan.

"José's obsession with trophies shone through," Carrick has recalled. "He was desperate to win the Community Shield to get us in the winning habit, [which led to two more trophies]. José just sees a way to win them."

Above Robin van Persie celebrates with Michael Carrick and Rafael da Silva after scoring against Aston Villa at Old Trafford in April 2013

In the summer of 2015 Van Gaal was backed again in the transfer market with the signings of Memphis Depay, Morgan Schneiderlin, Bastian Schweinsteiger and Anthony Martial, and while they helped United reach the top of the Premier League by the end of September, it was not to last.

Van Gaal's reign effectively came to an end with three consecutive defeats to Bournemouth, Norwich City and Stoke City in December, but he limped on until the end of the season as United looked for his replacement.

The Dutchman preached the importance of possession, but this involved too many backward passes. The Old Trafford crowd regularly grew restless, chanting "attack, attack, attack!" after being forced to sit through 11 consecutive games without a first-half goal. By the end of the season, United had scored only 49 goals – their lowest total for 26 seasons – to finish a disappointing fifth.

When Van Gaal did enjoy some success, it came too late; he guided United to their 12th FA Cup win with a 2-1 victory over

With the summer signings of Victor Lindelöf, Nemanja Matić and Romelu Lukaku for a combined £145 million, plus Alexis Sánchez, who arrived from Arsenal in the January, United enjoyed a better season in 2017–18, lifting themselves up to second behind a rampant Manchester City. A gap of 19 points between the two sides showed there was never a serious title race, so United's greatest pleasure was a 3-2 comeback win over City at the Etihad Stadium in April to stop them winning the title in front of them.

In the summer of 2018, Mourinho believed he needed more than just the signings of Fred and Diogo Dalot to launch a title challenge and was disappointed not to also add a new central defender to the ranks.

Any momentum from the previous season was frittered away as United lost five of their first 17 league games, and with United languishing in sixth, Mourinho was sacked after a 3-1 defeat to Liverpool at Anfield in December 2018. He would later admit that at this point he had deserved to lose his job.

United's first choice to replace Mourinho was the Tottenham Hotspur manager Mauricio Pochettino, but knowing they could not lure him from North London halfway through the season, the club brought in their former player Ole Gunnar Solskjaer on an interim basis until the end of the season. The appointment was something of a surprise, for Solskjaer appeared not to have enough experience for the role, having only managed Molde in his native Norway – ranked as the 21st best league in Europe – and Cardiff City, who were relegated from the Premier League under him in 2014.

However, the arrival of a club legend would breathe new life into the United squad, who went on a run of 14 wins from 17 games, including a dramatic 3-2 aggregate win over Paris Saint-Germain in the Champions League round of 16.

Left Phil Jones and Sir Alex Ferguson react to hearing the news Manchester City have scored a late winner to steal the 2012 title away from them
Below Ole Gunnar Solskjaer speaks to Marcus Rashford after a 4-2 defeat to Leicester City in October 2021

A giddy United board prematurely made Solskjaer their permanent manager with a three-year contract in March 2019 and then watched in horror as United's form slumped with four defeats from their final seven league games.

United began the following season with a stirring opening day 4-0 win over Chelsea, but by March 2020, when the Premier League shut down due to the Covid-19 pandemic, United had lost a total of eight league games. After a three-month break United returned as a new team, however, going unbeaten for the final nine league games of the season to finish third and reach the semi-finals of both the Europa League and FA Cup.

Playing in empty stadiums as the pandemic continued to grip the world, United were 15th after six games of the 2020–21 season, which included a sobering 6-1 defeat to José Mourinho's Tottenham Hotspur at Old Trafford. They were also knocked out of the Champions League at the group stage.

Solskjaer was able to engineer an impressive revival, winning ten times in 13 games to reach the top of the table by January 2021, the first time they had been there since 2013. But United immediately got a bad dose of vertigo and were overtaken by Manchester City, who finished 12 points ahead of them.

The chance for Solskjaer to win his first trophy as United manager was spurned when his side lost the Europa League final to Villarreal in a penalty shoot-out in Gdańsk after the game had finished 1-1 after extra-time.

This run to the final and their runners-up finish in the league, aligned with the summer signings of Jadon Sancho and Raphaël Varane, and the return of Cristiano Ronaldo in the summer, produced genuine excitement that United were finally ready to launch a sustained title challenge. Yet Solskjaer singularly failed to inspire the most talented squad United had boasted for at least a decade, and after a run of five defeats in seven league games – including an appalling 5-0 defeat to Liverpool at Old Trafford and a 4-1 capitulation at Watford – he was sacked in November.

The United goalkeeper David de Gea described the defeat to Watford as "embarrassing" and "another nightmare", and in a damning indictment of Solskjaer admitted, "We don't know what to do with the ball, we are conceding a lot of goals."

For the second time in three years, United found themselves stranded in mid-season with no hope of luring away their preferred candidate for new full-time manager, and so they had to make do with another interim, the highly experienced German coach Ralf Rangnick. It was a appointment that ultimately didn't work for either party, but in the summer of 2022 United finally secured a long-term successor to Solskjaer when they swooped for Ajax's Erik ten Hag.

After a tricky start, the Dutchman has since restored discipline and, most importantly, hope to Old Trafford. His no-nonsense approach and fluid style of play has fans daring to dream of silverware and a return to the glory days of old.

OWEN QUIETENS THE NOISY NEIGHBOURS

United remained the leading team in Manchester after a dramatic last-gasp derby win over City

In September 2009, after a pulsating 96 minutes that had witnessed United beating their neighbours Manchester City 4-3 in a classic Premier League fixture at Old Trafford, Sir Alex Ferguson hailed it as the "best derby of all time".

For the previous two decades United had been the dominant force in the city, but, after being bought by wealthy new owners, City believed they were finally ready to topple them.

In the build-up Ferguson and the City manager Mark Hughes traded hostile words, with both men keenly aware of what was at stake in this game.

United took the lead after two minutes through Wayne Rooney before Gareth Barry quickly equalised. In the second half, Darren Fletcher put United back in front, only for Craig Bellamy to draw City level again.

United thought they had won it when Fletcher scored his second goal with ten minutes remaining, but Bellamy capitalised on a mistake by Rio Ferdinand to make it 3-3 in the 90th minute to secure what City thought was a valuable point.

But in the sixth minute of added time Michael Owen received a pass from Ryan Giggs in front of the Stretford End and poked the ball past Shay Given to win it for United.

"It all happened in a spilt second," Owen recalled. "The target was tiny. The odds were stacked against me. The first touch was bob-on. I hit it, a straight prod with my right foot because that was all I could do, [I] thought, that's in… And then Old Trafford exploded."

"In the moments after the game, there was a feeling of joy. I'd scored an iconic goal. I knew that it was a moment I'd always be remembered for."

Getty Images

SHE DEVILS

Since its 2018–19 debut, the Manchester United Women's
team has become a force to be reckoned with

Words Michael E. Haskew

Above
Championship
winners in their
inaugural
season – not
a bad way to
kick off!

I t was a long time coming, but a wait that has proven worthwhile, and since the Manchester United Women's football team took the field for the first time during the 2018–19 season, they have written a chapter of tremendous achievement, pronounced restlessness and immense potential yet to be realised.

Their 13-year absence had been noticeable. One observer wrote in 2017, "...Manchester United will not release a women's team. They have been asked many times but refuse to do so... I don't agree with this because not only simply the fact that there should be a female side to Manchester, but also because all the other teams have one and would it really be that much of a struggle to make one... They could easily have a great team that would win all the time with the facilities and coaches available to them. It's not like Manchester can't afford to make a senior team..."

The presence and absence of a women's top-tier team wearing the bold red colours is a tale of once and future football prominence. From the late 1970s to 2001, the Manchester United Supporters Club Ladies actually served as something of a proxy for a vested senior women's football team. A founding club of the North West Women's Regional Football League in 1989, they competed through the 1990s in the FA Women's National League. In 2001, they formed a sanctioned partnership with Manchester United, but though it seemed the Club Ladies had hit their stride, there were [do]ldrums ahead.

[fin]ishes in the middle of the competitive pack had begun to turn [the]m stale, lacking real progress and intensity. By 2005, soon

after American industrialist and sports mogul Malcolm Glazer consolidated his ownership of Manchester United, the women's team was discontinued. The public discourse for its demise centred around a desire to concentrate on the Manchester United women's academy rather than a senior team, while simultaneously a women's senior programme was unprofitable and outside the core business emphasis of the ownership.

And so, for more than a decade, a discussion surrounding the renewal of a senior women's Manchester United team swirled. Then, in March 2018, the club formally announced its application to the FA to establish a team in the WSL2, a tier below their close rivals Manchester City in the new FA Women's Championship.

"After Real Madrid's application this year to create a women's team, United remained the only 'superclub' without one but are now catching up with pretty much every other English club in having a team that they plan to play at the club's training centre at The Cliff," reported Yahoo Sports at the time.

United's then Executive Vice-Chairman Ed Woodward commented, "The Manchester United Women's team must be built in the same image and with the same principles as the men's first team and offer academy players a clear route to top-level football within the club."

The Manchester United W.F.C. scored an electrifying coup with the hiring of Casey Stoney, a headlining defender with the England women's national football team, as well as Arsenal, Charlton Athletic, Chelsea, Lincoln and Liverpool during her senior career. Stoney was announced as the club's first head coach on 8 June 2018, and the team charged the field in August, winning their inaugural game 1-0 over Liverpool in the FA Women's League Cup, with veteran forward Lizzie Arnot scoring the team's first competitive goal in 13 years.

From there the club reached dizzying heights of success during their maiden campaign. Three weeks after that first victory, a 12-0 drubbing of Aston Villa served notice that United were going to be a force in the Championship. Sure enough promotion to the FA Super League came on 17 April 2019 after another victory over the claret and blue, this time 5-0. A 7-0 home win over Crystal Palace three days later sealed the FA Women's Championship crown. In May, Manchester United were named the FA Women's Championship Club of the Year.

The 2019–20 season was the first for United in the FA Women's Super League, and, on 7 September 2019, a 1-0 Manchester derby loss at rivals City drew an English domestic attendance record of 31,213. The following spring, the FA suspended the season temporarily due to the COVID-19 pandemic, and then ended it fully on 25 May 2020. Fourteen matches were played, and United were placed fourth in the WSL based on points per game.

As the 2020–21 season progressed, there were rumblings of discontent within United, despite the cheering news that the team had marked their Old Trafford debut with a 2-0 victory over West Ham and success on the Super League field had been steady. Still, FA League Cup performances had been frustrating, with a tie against Manchester City sandwiched between disheartening losses to Liverpool and Everton the previous autumn.

In May 2021, Stoney announced her resignation as head coach amid speculation that she was frustrated by lagging support from management, particularly in the allocation of resources to training facility improvement. The season ended with a second straight fourth-place finish, and blistering perspectives emerged in the news media.

One concerned reporter wrote, "Manchester United were expected to become one of the dominant forces in the women's game. But fast forward a couple of years, and the club has no manager, is losing key players rapidly, and is reportedly failing to provide high-quality facilities for its players."

Although the timeframe was lengthy – in fact more than two months – United ownership announced on 29 July 2021 that 38-year-old Marc Skinner, the experienced former manager of Birmingham City W.F.C and of the Orlando Pride of the National Women's Soccer League in the United States, would step into the sizable breach as head coach, signing a two-year contract with an option for a follow-on third.

The current campaign offers serious cause for optimism. After finishing fourth in the 2021–22 season, at the time of writing United currently sit at the top of the WSL table on 32 points, secured courtesy of ten wins, two draws and a single defeat to Chelsea, who are a point behind with a game in hand. The Londoners have won the last three league titles, but United are giving their illustrious rivals a real run for their money this season. The two sides will meet at Chelsea's home ground of Kingsmeadow on 12 March in what could be a title-deciding clash.

Marc Skinner's charges are still chasing silverware on two fronts after navigating their way to the fifth round of the Women's FA Cup. Up next are Durham of the Championship.

The team will only be five years old on the final day of the 2022–23 season, when United will travel to Liverpool's Prenton Park. There is growing belief that they might well mark the anniversary of their founding with a first-ever league title. Even if they don't quite pull it off, the sense that this talented side – recently bolstered by the addition of 21-year-old Canadian international defender Jayde Riviere, not to mention the retention of star striker Alessia Russo – is building something special at Leigh Sports Village is growing with every impressive victory. Marc Skinner is certainly very content with how his side is developing.

"I'm really happy with were the group are at, but we go game to game and we always will," he said after a recent 2-1 away win at Spurs. "The fans deserve to see their team at the top of the table."

If United continue on this trajectory, those fans might just need to get used to seeing their side top of the league on a regular basis.

"THEY WON THEIR INAUGURAL GAME, AND FROM THERE THE CLUB REACHED DIZZYING HEIGHTS DURING THEIR MAIDEN CAMPAIGN"

Right Marc Skinner, head coach of Manchester United Women, lays a wreath in remembrance of the Munich Air Disaster prior to a game against Everton at Leigh Sports Village, 5 February 2023

Bottom United and England striker Alessia Russo. The Euro 2022 winner has scored 17 goals for United in 37 games. In January 2023 Arsenal submitted two world-record bids for Russo, both of which were rejected

Images Getty, Wiki Images

THEY SAY NEVER GO BACK:
THE RISE AND
FALL OF RONALDO

Cristiano Ronaldo's second coming in Manchester couldn't
promise silverware, but it was certainly box office

Words Mark White

3

p.m. on a Saturday used to be sacred. It was the one time of day that English football would be played – until, of course, modern football moved to midweek evenings, Monday nights, Friday nights and every time slot in between. For so long since the advent of 24-hour rolling news and the Premier League becoming the product it is today, the 3 p.m. kick-off has been an easily ignorable one. The silent slot between the lunchtime and evening drama.

Not on 11 September 2021, however. The Rainy City drew to a standstill, and much of the world aligned its watches with Manchester's in anticipation. Cristiano Ronaldo was home. He'd sold more jerseys with this move, apparently, than Lionel Messi did when he moved to Paris Saint-Germain. And he was here to put on a show.

In 2003, it was Bolton Wanderers on a sunny afternoon. Then just a leggy teen, his teeth not yet straightened and with flecks of blonde in his hair, Ronaldo dazzled and danced through the opposition, bringing a box of tricks from Lisbon to England. This time Newcastle United were the opponents, and this time Ronaldo took to the field as returning king.

In the time between leaving English shores and coming back to the same club 12 years later, Ronaldo had transformed from one of the biggest talents of a particular generation into one of the most adored human beings the sport had ever seen. While some wither in the spotlight of Madrid, CR7 had garnered godlike status, winning five Champions League titles, leading his country to their first international trophy and scoring goals at a rate that no one had in the modern game (well, no one apart from a certain Argentine).

Right Happier times: the 2-1 win against West Ham in September 2021, secured courtesy of a late Jesse Lingard strike, showed Ronaldo at his lethal best

"THESE EARLY WEEKS WERE FEEL-GOOD, BUT AS THE DAYS GREW SHORTER SO DID THE PATIENCE, AS UNITED'S SQUAD OF SUPERSTAR TALENTS STRUGGLED TO GEL"

Left Deep in conversation with Raphaël Varane during Brighton's 2-1 victory at Old Trafford on the opening weekend of the 2022–23 season

But even including Messi, no one in football history has arguably played at 100 per cent of their ability quite so often as Cristiano Ronaldo had done before rejoining Manchester United. 450 goals in fewer Real Madrid games was testament to that. Every season he was in Spain, he scored over 30 goals a season – twice over 60 – before going to Juventus to conquer Italy. No one had ever scored more goals for Real. In his return at United, he made sure that no one would have ever scored more goals, full stop.

And it all began once more exactly how you'd imagine: a brace against a Newcastle side who wanted to curl up and wish the 90 minutes over as soon they began. Ronaldo leapt skyward and Old Trafford bellowed the customary 'Siu' in unison with their hero. He was back, all right – and the Premier League wasn't to be the same...

—

The rumours were that Cristiano Ronaldo was unhappy in Turin. Despite devastating defences deep into his 30s in Italy, Juventus were not a better team for acquiring the superstar after his fifth Champions League triumph with Real Madrid in 2018. The Old Lady crashed out of the competition to Ajax, then Lyon, then Porto. It was hardly befitting.

Manchester City were rumoured to be interested in the Portuguese poacher as their Plan B after a summer of chasing Harry Kane, but rumours of Ronaldo working under Pep Guardiola served only to

motivate their city rivals to seal a deal. It felt right: Ole Gunnar Solskjaer had played with Ronaldo and now he'd brought him back home – for roughly the same fee that United had originally paid for him – to complete his team. This was a squad that had finished second to City the season prior, runner-up in the Europa League, and in the eyes of many, all they really needed was that superstar difference-maker.

Two goals on his second debut certainly set the tone before Ronaldo netted against Young Boys in the Champions League. The weekend after, West Ham simply couldn't contain his movement and again, Ronaldo found a way. This victory was followed by a narrow 1-0 loss to Aston Villa that witnessed a rare Bruno Fernandes penalty miss, triggered in no small part by the mind games of Villa keeper Emi Martinez. In his head, Ronaldo was chalking that one up as one he'd have slotted home with ease.

His home bow in the Champions League showed just why United had brought him back. In a group game against Villarreal (who United had toiled against in the Europa League final the season before, desperately trying to carve them open to no avail before a heartbreaking penalty-shootout loss) it seemed that once again the Yellow Submarine's safety hatch would remain firmly bolted shut. Solksjaer's boys pelted the Spaniards, who defended resolutely in their two blocks of four. And then, four minutes into time added on, Ronaldo finally intervened, slotting home to snatch a crucial 2-1 win and unleash euphoria inside Old Trafford.

It summed up the mood of that time. These early weeks of the season were feel-good, fans buoyed by the nostalgia of how they felt with Ronaldo in tow first time around: the hope, the expectation, but mainly just the joy of being in his presence after all he'd achieved in the game. But as the days grew shorter so did the patience, as United's huge squad of superstar talents struggled to gel as one. Solskjaer had survived scrapes before as manager but never fully enjoyed the unanimous trust that he was the man to believe in.

A miserable 4-2 loss to Leicester was compounded by a 5-0 drubbing to Liverpool and a 2-0 loss to City at home, in which United showed just how far they were from being challengers. Ronaldo had shone in a 3-0 win against Tottenham, with Solskjaer reverting to a

back three, but a dismal Watford side battered United 4-1 just a few weeks later. The writing was now on the wall for the Norwegian.

It left United – and Ronaldo – in a strange position. The Red Devils had signed what they believed to be the final piece of the jigsaw, only to realise weeks into the season that the picture they were working towards was all wrong. Ronaldo was here to elevate a top team, not to help a side in transition to negotiate a sticky period. And with uncertainty in the air, United hired Red Bull visionary Ralf Rangnick: a man who'd coached for just two seasons of the previous ten. They were about to embark on a bold new direction.

—

Rangnick was in the house to watch Ronaldo turn on the style against Arsenal. The Gunners were young but in impressive form: CR7 had been the difference-maker historically when this pair clashed at the top of the table, and once more, he hit the rewind button.

The game was end-to-end, fast and frenetic, with the Portuguese superstar making his presence count with another two goals. As Rangnick folded his programme into his pocket at full-time, a wry smile on his face, there was hope that if he could improve the rest of the outfit around the likes of Ronaldo, Jadon Sancho, Marcus Rashford and Bruno Fernandes, United could find themselves in contention once more.

Top left A bemused Ronaldo receiving instruction from Erik ten Hag during a loss to Aston Villa
Top right Ronaldo at his wits end – a familiar sight in his second spell at United – this time against Brighton
Above Ronaldo with partner Georgina Rodríguez and friend/confidant Piers Morgan
Left Ronaldo is unveiled as an Al-Nassr player as the saga over his future draws to a close once and for all

Perhaps United underestimated just how in flux they really were. There was no constant in the Rangnick reign, as formations came and went, players came in and dropped out, while fans questioned who could be relied on. Ronaldo was visibly annoyed at being substituted against Brentford in a 3-1 win – and for the first time in his career, question marks were raised about whether he was actually helping his team or not. He didn't seem to press very much, though some claimed that it didn't matter, so long as he delivered goals. And he certainly did that.

Ronaldo finished as top scorer with 24 strikes in all competitions, and there were plenty of highlights, as towards the end of the season he went on his customary run of obliterating defences for fun. Tottenham were destroyed en route to the top four, with Ronaldo netting a spectacular hat-trick, toying with defenders and proving just how devastating he could be in the big games. In netting the 807th

"THIS WAS A PROCESS, ONE THAT RONALDO COULDN'T WAIT AROUND TO BE A PART OF. SO HE TOOK MATTERS INTO HIS OWN HANDS"

goal of his career, he became the FIFA-recognised all-time top goalscorer in the sport, and in his 83 minutes, he was easily the best player on the pitch. He netted another three against Norwich, then scored against Arsenal, Brentford and Chelsea. He was irrepressible, despite criticism. But it came at a cost. Marcus Rashford's form dropped off a cliff and rumours began to swirl that he could leave his boyhood club. Bruno Fernandes' inability to perform at the same time as Ronaldo came into light – the attacking midfielder also shone in his countryman's absence – while Jadon Sancho's first season in the Premier League was deemed a disappointment.

Sure, Ronaldo was scoring goals, but some argued that there was more to a modern forward that he neglected to offer.

When United dropped out of the Champions League in the last 16, it felt symbolic. Atlético Madrid, forever whipping boys for Ronaldo, were the team to knock them out, with the perennial thorn in their side registering 0xG. It felt like the end of an era. With United failing to qualify for the competition, Ronaldo would have either played his last game in the competition he'd made his own or he'd have to leave once more.

—

You either die a hero or live long enough to realise that actually you should have included a break clause in your two-year contract. With United finishing sixth in the Premier League and Ronaldo coming under more scrutiny than ever, it became almost impossible for the Portuguese to move to a Champions League club.

That was what he wanted. Incoming manager Erik ten Hag insisted that he wanted Ronaldo around, but in limited displays the same sulkiness was apparent. The cameras all converged on his frustrated face during the 4-0 embarrassment away to Brentford, and he stormed off before full-time during a 2-0 win over Spurs at Old Trafford in late October. Ten Hag was more than happy to play without his star forward – and United looked better when he did.

It became very clear very quickly that he is not the kind of player you sign when you need patience. As United's new-look side took shape, with CR7's former Real Madrid team-mate Casemiro slotting in, Antony joining and Rashford finding his feet once more as a key component. Ten Hag's boys were beginning to ball. Wins over Liverpool and Arsenal, however, were spliced with set-backs to Aston Villa and Manchester City, the latter a 6-3 mauling. This was a process, one that Ronaldo, 37, couldn't wait around to be a part of. So he took matters into his own hands.

The forward's interview with superfan Piers Morgan may go down as one of the most bizarre ways a player has ever cut ties with their club. Rather than going on strike or handing in a transfer request, Ronaldo waited until the Premier League season had paused for World Cup duty before slamming his employers' decision-making, declaring he had "no respect" for his manager and saying he felt "betrayed". Essentially, he forced United to terminate his contract.

The fury and confusion was palpable. Here was a club legend severing all ties in the most public way possible. It felt utterly unnecessary to some, but in some ways it was pure Ronaldo. A move to Al-Nassr in Saudi Arabia followed, facilitated not by veteran agent Jorge Mendes but by lawyers. United fans began chanting, "I don't care about Ronnie". The reunion had only lasted around 15 months in the end. Like the man itself, it had burned bright and it was impossible to ignore.

While some players in recent seasons at Old Trafford have found their motivation doesn't match their mobility, Ronaldo's biggest fault was the opposite. The insatiable hunger to score goals at the highest level was something he wasn't even willing to compromise for the club that had made him what he is today. They knew exactly what they were getting, and some will even still say now that they'd rather have that than some of the flops of recent years.

The dust is settling now, though. Ronaldo is the biggest thing in Saudi Arabia, recently netting four times in the same match, and his story is far from finished. He is still only 38. Perhaps United and its prodigal son will reconcile again one day. For all the great memories – even the second time around – it would be a shame if they didn't.

DUTCH COURAGE

THE ERIK TEN HAG ERA

Could he be the man to restore glory to the Theatre of Dreams?

Words Steve Wright

The arrival of Erik ten Hag at Manchester United came in the wake of something the Old Trafford faithful had become accustomed to over the previous nine seasons: failure.

It's fair to say that the 2021–22 season was one to forget. Coming off the back of a respectable second-place finish and a Europa Cup final (admittedly a drab defeat to Villarreal), manager Ole Gunnar Solskjaer initially seemed to have buried the ghosts of Gdansk with four wins from the opening five games. However, this was followed by five defeats in the next seven, with an embarrassing 4-1 reverse at Watford proving to be the final straw, and Solskjaer was duly jettisoned.

The Old Trafford hierarchy didn't exactly cover themselves in glory with their next appointment. Ralf Rangnick was drafted in, but with it being made clear that this was to be an interim appointment, they remained inconsistent. The results were early exits in the cups and a 6th-place league finish.

With Rangnick's contract up, the search was on for someone who could succeed where Moyes, Van Gaal, Mourinho and Solskjaer had failed. As you would expect from one of the world's most famous clubs, big names were linked – Mauricio Pochettino featuring most prominently. Rather than appointing yet another manager who had bounced between Europe's top clubs, however, they looked towards a rising star.

Erik ten Hag had worked his way up. Having retired early from playing during a modest career in the Dutch leagues, he spent a year in charge at Go Ahead Eagles before making the move to Germany to manage Bayern Munich's 'B' team under future rival Pep Guardiola. After two years here he returned to the Netherlands to take charge of former club Utrecht, who he successfully steered towards European qualification before taking on the mantle at the country's top club: Ajax.

'Outsiders' don't always have the best track record at Ajax, but it's testament to ten Hag that he bucked this trend, guiding the Amsterdam-based giants to three title wins, two KNVB Cups and to within seconds of a Champions League final, a glittering tenure that attracted the attention of many of Europe's leading clubs, including the top brass at Old Trafford.

The challenge he now faces in Manchester is bigger than any he has known before. There is the financial clout of Manchester City, Chelsea and now Newcastle to contend with, as well as a resurgent Arsenal, and Liverpool and Tottenham sides helmed by past Premier League winners Jürgen Klopp and Antonio Conte.

Yet, judging by his comments to Sky Sports upon his appointment, ten Hag 'gets' what it is to be at Man United, and his place in the scheme of things: "We don't have to go over my football," he said when asked about his playing style. "It's about the Man United football and about the Man United identity and philosophy… We have to bring structures in the way of playing, so we can play attacking football." Indeed, it helped that he restored a link to the Alex Ferguson days by bringing along his former assistant Steve McClaren (who ten Hag worked under at Twente).

Indeed, much like Ferguson was famed for having influence over every aspect of life at Old Trafford, ten Hag goes beyond picking the team. He has insisted on being in full control of the U23 squad to ensure a better pathway into the first team, as well as banning players from employing personal chefs in order to more closely monitor their diet.

He also hasn't been afraid to change the order of things. Over his opening six months ten Hag raided his old club for centre-back Lisandro Martínez and winger Antony, splashing out £56.7m and £86m respectively. Another new face was found in the form of Dutch left-back Tyrell Malacia, signed from Feyenoord for £12.9m. After an unsuccessful pursuit of Barcelona's Frenkie de Jong, a replacement was found in the form of Casemiro from Real Madrid for £70m, before a productive window was rounded off by the arrival of Christian Eriksen on a free transfer.

Images Getty Images

Yet while he had been backed in the transfer market, results didn't come straight away for ten Hag. Despite a promising pre-season campaign that included victories over Liverpool and Atlético Madrid, the opening couple of games couldn't have gone much worse: his Man United debut – home to Brighton on 7 August - finished in a 2-1 defeat thanks to goals from Pascal Gross.

Worse was to come the following week, as ten Hag's charges were battered 4-0 by Brentford at the Gtech Community Stadium. All four goals came during the opening 35 minutes, with United having no answer to the workmanlike Bees.

The knives were already out, with new signing Martínez singled out. Short for a centre-back at 5ft 9in, those questioning whether he would be able to physically compete at the top level of English football were given further ammunition after watching him get outmuscled by Ben Mee for Brentford's third.

But ten Hag stuck to his guns. The following game against Liverpool saw a number of changes: while Martínez retained his place, England internationals Harry Maguire and Luke Shaw were dropped, as was Cristiano Ronaldo, who would remain in a bit-part role for the remainder of his Man United career. In the end, ten Hag's changes were vindicated, as they ran out 2-1 winners thanks to goals from Jadon Sancho and Marcus Rashford (both much improved after disappointing campaigns the previous year), with Martínez repaying his manager's faith by keeping Mohamed Salah quiet for much of the game and Malacia justifying his inclusion ahead of Shaw.

The next few weeks saw them put a solid run together that banished their early season woes. A second-half Bruno Fernandes volley secured a 1-0 at Southampton before former champions Leicester were beaten by the same score a few days later. Antony then marked his debut by opening the scoring in a 3-1 home defeat of Arsenal, the Brazilian's strike followed by a brace from Rashford.

Right Celebrating a crucial 2-1 victory over Manchester City in January 2023

Far right Ten Hag welcomes Antony, having pushed hard for his signature

"TEN HAG DESERVES CREDIT FOR INSPIRING THE BULK OF THE SQUAD TO IMPROVE"

Left Ten Hag has had to act ruthlessly, not least by dropping Cristiano Ronaldo

After a brief Europa League interlude (a 1-0 defeat and 2-0 victory against Real Sociedad and Sheriff Tiraspol respectively), they were brought back down to earth in brutal fashion in a 6-3 hammering away to Man City; two strikes from Anthony Martial and Antony proving little consolation in the wake of hat-tricks for both Erling Haaland and Phil Foden. It was a marker of the level that they were still some way short of.

They quickly got over it, however; successive wins against Omonia Nicosia in the Europa League bookended a 2-1 away win at Everton, with Antony adding to his tally and Ronaldo notching his 700th career goal. They would remain unbeaten throughout the rest of October, recording stalemates against Newcastle and Chelsea (during which Casemiro recorded his first goal in United colours), as well as a 2-0 triumph over Tottenham courtesy of strikes from Fred and Fernandes, a Rashford-powered 1-0 triumph over West Ham, and another Europa League triumph over Sheriff Tiraspol.

November was more mixed, as they achieved revenge over Real Sociedad with a 1-0 victory thanks to youngster Alejandro Garnacho (the recipient of more game time after impressing ten Hag). On the other hand, they were shocked by Aston Villa 3-1 at Villa Park, a Jacob Ramsey own goal their only consolation as they went down to a side enjoying an Unai Emery-powered new manager bounce. A 4-2 victory over Villa a few days later in the League Cup (Martial, Rashford, Fernandes and Scott McTominay the scorers) was slight consolation, before heading into the World Cup break on a high thanks to a narrow 2-1 victory over Fulham (thanks to Eriksen and Garnacho).

Their return saw them pick up where they left off, defeating Burnley in the League Cup before recording four straight league victories: 3-1 at home to Nottingham Forest (Martial, Rashford, Fred);

1-0 away at Wolves (Rashford, coming off the bench); 3-0 against Bournemouth (Casemiro, Shaw, Rashford); and, most gratifyingly, a coming-of-age performance in a 2-1 home triumph over Man City, with Fernandes (somewhat controversially) and Rashford sealing the deal after going behind to Jack Grealish. They continued their cup advance with a 3-1 victory over Everton in the FA Cup, and ten Hag became the quickest Man United manager to hit 20 victories with a 3-0 League Cup quarter-final win over Charlton.

Even so, work still clearly has to be done. Missing the suspended Casemiro, ten Hag's charges lost 3-2 to league leaders Arsenal at the Emirates, a 90th-minute Eddie Nketiah tap in snatching all three points for the Gunners in a game that had seen the visitors leading through Rashford and later pulling level at 2-2 via a Martínez header. With United currently sitting third in the table five points behind Arsenal (who have played two games less) and three behind second-placed Man City, a title charge may not be out of the question, although it would require quite a collapse from Arteta's men.

Regardless, ten Hag deserves huge credit for inspiring the bulk of United's squad to improve and instilling his drive and determination into the team. Rashford is back to his best, embracing the rewards that come with being more direct, Dalot has embraced consistency, and Raphaël Varane is finally looking like a World Cup winner. Even players who initially found themselves out of favour, like Luke Shaw and Aaron Wan-Bissaka, have shown that there's a pathway back into the team. While they've commanded substantial fees, it can't be denied that the likes of Antony, Martínez, Malacia and Casemiro have justified the outlay.

He's not without his ruthless side, however, as shown by the events that led to Ronaldo's departure, as well as dropping Rashford for the Wolves game due to disciplinary matters. Moreover, Harry Maguire has largely found himself out in the cold, with left-back Shaw being preferred to him at centre-back in recent weeks.

While ten Hag has a lot to do before he brings the glory days back to Old Trafford, there is no doubt that he has allowed fans to dream once more.

Images Getty Images